BORNE
FROM
ABOVE

BORNE FROM ABOVE

A Spiritual Journey
with Carnal Detours

ERNEST KOLOWRAT

"The word of God is alive and active. It is sharper than any double-edged sword. It cuts all the way through, to where soul and spirit meet, to where joints and marrow come together. It judges the desires and thoughts of our hearts.
– St. Paul to the Hebrews

If we are destined to wise up eventually,
why not wise up now? "

– J. A. Comenius (1592-1670)

PROLOGUE
FALL 1955

"We take it for granted that our experience here on earth is supposed to be enjoyable, that it is our birthright to derive pleasure from daily life. Gentlemen, this assumption blithely ignores the evidence."

On the podium was Professor Franklin Le Van Baumer, delivering one of his three weekly lectures to our intellectual history class during my junior year at Yale. A tall, distinguished-looking scholar, Professor Baumer liked to gesticulate vehemently when his back wasn't hurting him. With his lumbago acting up, he was careful to make no untoward move. "There is no guarantee," he continued stiffly, "that our unexpected freak of history, when enjoyment of life is considered the norm, is assured any kind of a future. Virtually all of history, as well as the abject conditions in which most of humanity lives today, point strongly against it."

Our professor's prognosis resonated through the cavernous neo-Gothic hall but failed to strike a responsive chord. The unbounded optimism I held as an article of faith wasn't going to be affected by a few dire words. It certainly augured well that as a recent refugee from behind the Iron Curtain I already found myself with a scholarship at Yale. Most of my friends here were sanguine about the future too, and not just because they were at Yale. Why, even in the blighted parts of the world people were leading better lives. Was Professor Baumer so isolated in his intellectual lair that he failed to understand the world in which he lived? Or was the professor's aching back more likely to blame? A permanent cure would surely brighten his views! And I wondered, why was it that so many of the great thinkers across the ages had some physical problem or mental quirk affecting the ideas with which they tried to saddle the world? Saint Augustine went around for years moaning, "God, make me chaste . . . but not yet!" — and then did his utmost to inflict the dubious blessings of his celibacy on everyone else. Was it because his personal ardor for intimate pleasures had waned? Having myself just turned twenty, this was a problem I could hardly understand. And I had an exciting thought. What if the world were to come under the sway of a philosophy formulated by someone who had a healthy appetite for life? I was the 175-pound intramural boxing champion, yet I had pretty good grades. Why couldn't I figure out a valid philosophical system for our times that would one day be taught in Professor Baumer's class — or at least be included on the optional reading list? It was a thought with which I occasionally liked to entertain myself, especially after a few beers at the Old Heidelberg bar.

It was also a thought that would remain with me to this day.

PART ONE
DECEMBER 1978

1/

It was a little after seven when I awoke to a gray midwinter
dawn, the lower panes of the half-open window covered with
frost. The small radiator clattering under the sill was hardly sufficient to heat the frigid air rolling in as visible sheets of mist.

I took refuge deeper in the warmth of my bed; oh, to have
just a moment more within this pleasurable retreat! Then I made
the lunge to release the latch that let the window down.

I could feel the room start warming up. It was a small room,
but it had remained mine all these years I had been coming back
to stay at my parents' Massachusetts farmhouse. On one wall
hung a permanent display of some of the more illustrious ancestors from Father's side, clad in fine silk robes of confidants at
royal courts, or in gilded military uniforms suggestive of heroic
deeds. On another wall were several framed photographs depict-
ing cherished moments from my past, including one on the beach
in Lignano, Italy, walking arm-in-arm with the eye-catching
wife of a noted Austrian prince. The biggest photo of the lot had
been taken more than a decade ago by an alluring shoe heiress

from Saint Louis, who had balked at marrying me for fear of falling into immediate penury. The poster-sized rendition showed me standing on the pink sands of Bermuda's Elbow Beach, with every muscle delineated almost as well as when I had boxed as a light-heavyweight at Yale. I was slimmer now but the muscles were still there. It was a standard from which I was determined not to retreat for as long as I could.

This was usually my favorite time in bed, when I could roll over and nap, waiting for the room to become pleasantly warm. I was vaguely aware of Father downstairs going through his morning exercise routine. He was over eighty now and continued to do justice to his honorific title of Mr. Exercycle. With his commanding presence and distinctive features hinting at youthful energy, he could still charm most women at will, especially if it meant selling one of his conditioning machines. I could hear him doing leg raises, banging his heels rhythmically on the floor.

I wasn't having much success falling back to sleep. Moving around in bed, I was feeling strangely restless as if I wasn't completely myself, as if a part of me had been taken over by something that didn't belong. I had never felt this way before and wondered: was this what male menopause was all about? There were other tip offs, too. I had been beset lately by dreams of missing trains, usually at one of the great European stations like the Hauptbahnhof in Munich or the Gare de L'Est in Paris. Dashing with my bags through the crowds along a seemingly endless boarding platform, I would watch the rear car disappearing beyond the maze of winding tracks, leaving me alone on the deserted platform.

I sat up abruptly with an unwelcome thought. Had I passed my prime, and somewhere along the line missed the waiting train? Indeed, I had recently scaled down my aspirations.

Instead of further massaging the prose of *Future Pleasure* (my meanderings about humanity's ultimate destiny on earth) in the hope of having it published, I took on a series of film scripts for a producer in Miami on daycare centers in the Southeast. The money promised to be good, but the job would be tedious and extend over several months, which was far longer than I could expect to sleep on my brother's couch in his little North Miami house. This had led me to a drastic step. After nearly a decade of a peripatetic existence, I had signed a one-year lease for an apartment of my own. It was in an attractive modern building at the water's edge of Miami's vaunted Coconut Grove. Yet rather than being relieved over this constructive step, I felt as if I had fallen into a trap. My dream had been to settle in California, preferably Laguna Beach. Years ago, as a Navy ensign, I used to return to my ship from weekends at this ocean-side retreat, reinvigorated, as if I had been swimming in chilled champagne. More recently, the famous octogenarian naturopath from nearby San Juan Capistrano, Dr. Henry Bieler, had helped me regain my health with his uncompromising, zucchini-based diet. Surely the place would have worked its magic once more and lifted me out of the latest doldrums! But alas, California would have to wait. While I hadn't moved into my Florida apartment yet, I had been driving there every few days from my brother's house to literally take on the fleas left behind by the previous tenant with a Siamese cat. I didn't want the management to use any of those sprays that would deposit a poisonous residue. My own method consisted of placing a bear rug I owned in the middle of the empty living room and leaving it there for several days until I returned. In the absence of a cat, the furry rug attracted the forsaken fleas. I would then take off my shoes and socks and walk back and forth on the rug, providing an opportunity for the fleas to jump on my warm ankles and calves. This they did in droves; I would then pick them off by hand and dispose of them down the toilet. During each visit, I repeated the rug-walking procedure several times, eventually tempting even the most recalcitrant to take the fatal leap. In the process, I met an airline stewardess who held a long-term lease on an apartment only two doors down from where I was going to live. Her smile seemed to be as beckoning as in that famous *Fly Me!* advertising campaign, and before long, she invited me to dinner at her place. As we sipped glass after glass of champagne, I tried to caution her that I might not be a good prospect for a sustained affair. I even implied I was the immature superficial type partial to passionate sex. I suspected already from the way she kissed that she had never experienced passionate sex and probably never would. Where would that leave me for the duration of my lease? As soon as the champagne wore off, I found out. Coming to with a start at her side in bed, I felt distressed over what I had done and tried to sneak out without waking her up. But in the dark, I couldn't find my pants. I fell fitfully asleep again for an hour or so, and then tried to make a discreet exit once more under the cover of the night. This time, I found my pants but couldn't find my socks and shoes. Nevertheless, I tiptoed out barefoot to my car parked downstairs in the apartment lot, and with great relief fled the scene. I spent the rest of the night on my brother's couch, and phoned the stewardess the following morning with a plausible explanation for my vanishing act. But I had yet to return to pick up my shoes or launch any further missions against the fleas.

Contemplating this episode at my parents' Massachusetts home, I realized there was no way I could fall asleep now. How did I manage to get so messed up, I wondered half aloud. I didn't blame the stewardess and still felt terrible about the way I had behaved. Her misfortune was to have been the first since my breakup with Katherine, a promising literary agent who had balked at handling the *Future Pleasure* manuscript but embraced its author with resolute abandon. In my continuing quest for the ideal bride, she set a new standard, combining a tenderness of character with a tumultuous physicality that propelled us into a special dimension of our own. The realization that I might never find another partner with Katherine's attributes was at least in part causing my depression – along with the prospects of those boring day care scripts, the apartment I didn't want, and the stewardess I dreaded to face.

The room felt sufficiently warm, and I jumped out of bed. Quick, do your exercise; a brisk ten minutes of deep-knee bends, pushups and sit-ups, capped by running a foot-long rubber roller vigorously over my muscles from head to toe for several minutes. The roller had multiple rows of red suction cups and little rubber prongs, which made it look like something for internal use from a porno shop. Years ago, while living in a communal East Side brownstone in New York, the motherly maid who came in from Harlem once a week had boiled my previous version of this device, thinking it needed to be sterilized. On a subsequent trip to Europe, I had to make a special trip to Munich to buy a replacement in the only store which carried that line. Unlike the roller I had once bought in France, this one was perfectly machined with ball bearings that prevented it from snagging body hair. Maybe this unique instrument would help dispel the strange, forlorn feeling I hadn't been able to shake since waking up.

It was time for me to go to the kitchen. I could no longer hear the lunging and grunting while Father had shadow-boxed. The inviting aroma of coffee was drifting up to my room. Mother, as usual, would already have eaten, but Father would be breakfasting now. I truly enjoyed my parents and didn't want to think of a time when they wouldn't be around. Yet, I knew how inevitable that was, and even this perennial reflection started to suffuse me with unusual grief.

Father was pouring his last cup of coffee, already dressed in coat and tie for the drive to his Boston office. As I watched him add milk and stir in two spoonfuls of sugar, I noticed how vigorous and fresh he looked. Born to a gentle existence when the Austro-Hungarian Empire was still functioning, he had been an illustrious count with progressive views, an influential voice in politics, and a generous patron of the arts. His fortunes had abruptly changed when the Communists took over his country and confiscated his properties — including the first Renaissance palace in Prague and a quaint, ivy-covered castle in the woods of the former Sudetenland. Emigrating with his wife and five children to the United States, he was unceremoniously forced to learn how to fend for himself in the rough exposure to America's unprivileged ways. He had a number of abortive starts (our mortgaged farmhouse was what remained of several years of trying to run a milk business), and at times he despaired. How often had I seen Father crinkle his cheeks into a grimace that turned his eyes into slits! It took an endless decade before he finally found his niche selling Exercycles, with his exclusive franchise for New England. His most effective sales technique in recent years was to lug the 100-pound machine into somebody's home without being winded and then reveal his age. Father was reconciled with his lot, and his paramount aim now was to continue thwarting old age and sell enough of those exercise machines to promptly pay his bills.

"Your face looks kind of crumpled," Father observed jovially. "What's the matter, didn't you sleep well?"

"I slept just fine, thank you."

"I'm sure it's something in your head again. If you made a nice son or two, like I always told you to, you wouldn't be having these troubles. You can't spend all of your life just ficking around and have nothing to show for it. At least I'm glad I did the right thing . . . that I made all of you kids and married Mother."

This was Father's familiar refrain about how he had succeeded where I had failed. Married to a Russian princess who couldn't have children, Father had followed an alluring, young woman bursting with health onto a tram taking her to the outskirts of Prague, where her parents owned a butcher shop. Hampered by his reputation as a man-about-town, it took Father another five years before he managed to convince my mother-to-be of his serious fatherhood intent.

"Can't I please have my breakfast in peace?" I grumbled, as I finished squeezing two oranges and a grapefruit for my morning glass of juice. I was feeling vulnerable. Father's double-edged thrust served as a poignant reminder of what I had forfeited with Katherine. I found myself blinking fast, remembering the night she had leaned over me in bed, and thinking I was asleep, whispered, "Oh darling, I love you so terribly and want to marry you and have your babies!" While a part of me had wanted to respond, I instinctively withdrew deeper into that feigned sleep. As much as I felt for her, how could I forever remove myself from all other inviting possibilities in the world, especially if my career prospects were to start brightening again? Alas, it was only after she was irrevocably gone that I realized she was the ideal long-term partner I had been looking for.

I sat down across from Father and tried to concentrate on spooning out my two soft boiled eggs and slathering gobs of butter on my toast. Although Father had finished eating, he put another piece of bread in the toaster.

"All that butter! I don't know how you do it without getting fat," he said with grudging admiration. "I get hungry just watching you. I liked it better when you had your zucchini breakfast. Then I wasn't tempted at all. You know, in the old days, you would have made a great *Voresser*."

It wasn't the first time Father had ventured this opinion, and I knew what he meant. A Voresser was literally, one who eats before; usually a person of modest means hired by wealthy or noble families overstuffed with five daily meals and in need of an example to work up their appetites. Gorging himself in the presence of this haughty company, the Voresser received both an ample meal and a nominal fee.

"That would have solved your job problem," Father laughed, while he sparingly buttered his toast. "As a Voresser, you would have really enjoyed your work."

Despite the way I felt, I managed a feeble smile. I didn't notice Mother, who had materialized seemingly from nowhere in her fraying bathrobe. A gray-haired lady with deeply etched worry lines, she looked a bit hurt, as if Father-the-Count had inadvertently slighted one of her plebeian children, for whom she had sacrificed so much and held such high hopes.

"Voresser?" she asked with a touch of irony. "And for that he went to Yale?"

2/

I had come home for the week between Christmas and New Year's, and my stay was drawing to a close. I was glad this happened to be the day I had promised to visit my sister Manya on Cape Cod and spend the night at her house. Maybe the three-hour drive and change of scenery would help me find my old self again.

A year younger than I, my sister and I had a relationship dating back to when I was a three-year-old. That's when I had perfected the practice of snatching the pacifier out of her mouth while she was asleep and sticking it into mine. What had me hooked was the delicately tingling sensation of rotating my finger through the plastic safety ring on the opposite end. Of course, if my baby sister unexpectedly woke up and started to bawl, I would stick the pacifier back into her mouth, hoping she would fall asleep before Mother was alerted by her cries. A decade later as a thirteen-year-old, I was the one who revealed to his twelve-year-old sister (at that time attending a Catholic school with my younger sister Eve) the biological prerequisites for producing a child – a shocking activity whose necessity she was loath to recognize.

Now a strikingly attractive but deliberately sedate mother of five in her mid-forties, my sister lived in a comfortable house on the outskirts of a popular summer destination, where her husband was the manager of a large resort hotel. Manya welcomed my visits, despite her fear of the influence I might have on her children, especially her pert ten-year-old who strutted around in her John Lennon T-shirt, dreaming of a chance for a tryout in film or on stage. But Manya was willing to take the risk for the opportunity to give me a personal pitch on how Jesus could change my life. She remained undeterred by my oft-repeated stance that I wasn't about to have Jesus cramp my style, especially as interpreted by some horny celibates in the Catholic Church. I invariably begged off Manya's invitations to her charismatic prayer meetings, which she said were the key to anyone's spiritual life. "I guess I'm not ready yet," I always said smugly, preferring to sit around with her husband for another glass of wine while she went off after dinner to meet with her prayer group. "As you yourself say, "I would invariably add, "Jesus will let me know when the right time comes."

It was early afternoon by the time I left for the drive to the Cape in my little hatchback car. Having felt distraught throughout the day, I was glad to be alone with my thoughts. At least I didn't have to worry about Mother or anyone else seeing me in this sorry state. And indeed, it wasn't long before I found myself wiping an occasional dribble off my cheeks as I again yielded to involuntary self-flagellation over Katherine. I was anguishing over the time toward the end of our relationship when I had weaseled out of a promise that she could accompany me on a three-week skiing trip to the French Pyrenees. It wasn't a question of money, since she had offered to pay her way. But I wanted to include a weeklong visit at an aging aunt's rundown château at the foot of the mountains where I planned to ski. This would have exposed Katherine – or so I tried to convince her – to rats, bats, spiders and a whole array of other primitive conditions associated with fourteenth century dwellings. With a trace of sadness and a wan smile, she acquiesced. My real reason for wanting to travel alone was that I didn't want to be exposed to Katherine's increasingly depressed moods. Her stress pimple was becoming more prominent and she was seeing her psychiatrist twice a week. When I arrived at the Pyrenees skiing resort, I wrote her an exultant card, signing it, *Ever Singularly*. In our happier days, Katherine had often joked how different I was; singular is what she had called me. But seeing the word on my postcard, she took it the wrong way. When I returned a week later than she had expected, I could tell she was severely disturbed, despite being on Valium. That evening she haltingly confessed she had come close to turning on the gas, thinking I had left her for good. God, if I had only realized I was the source of her depression and could have lifted her out of it with a few well-chosen words! After several more days of gathering her strength, Katherine gave me up like a noxious drug. We were mismatched from the start, she calmly observed, as she asked for my set of keys to her apartment and wished me well.

Remembering the parting scene in the solitude of my car, I clutched the steering wheel with both hands. God, how I had screwed myself! Katherine had been willing to forgo a number of financially successful suitors for my sake, and I had balked at her proffered sacrifice. I suddenly recalled a remark by a casual friend who published ghoulish comic books featuring religious terror as their theme. "Being sorry for having screwed yourself is hardly a meaningful contrition," this self-proclaimed atheist had pointed out, with a mixture of sincerity and jest. "Nor is it enough to be contrite because you had screwed or offended somebody else. If you're to have any chance of being spared the fires of hell, you have to be sincerely and truly sorry for having offended God." I had tried at that time to dismiss those words as coming from a loon; now, as I continued the drive across the Bourne Bridge to the Cape, I was tormented with a distressing thought: Had I indeed offended God – not only with Katherine but throughout my life?

By the time I arrived at Manya's, I felt emotionally drained. Fortunately, dinner was waiting, and I was able to camouflage

my mood by concentrating on the food. I repeatedly compli-
mented my sister, if only for want of anything else to say, on the
evident care she had taken preparing the meal. Then, as we were
finishing dessert, Manya made her customary pitch. "There's a
prayer meeting tonight," she said, with the caution of a child
reaching out to a puppy that might bite. "Would you like to
come?"

I was, in fact, anticipating her request. I had always been the
type willing to try anything, the way I did with Dr. Bieler's zucchini cure for the breakdown of my health. Now, I was feeling on
the verge of a breakdown of a different sort; so why not give
Manya's salutary suggestion a chance?

The swiftness of my response took away my sister's breath.
"Sure," I said, as casually as I could. "Let's go."

3/

A balding, chunky man was conducting the prayer meeting. He
wore a shiny warm-up jacket over a heavy, red-checkered shirt.
He introduced himself as Al in a thick Boston accent that made
his every *a* sound as if it had been drawn out and pressed down.
My sister told me he was the local plumber.

Attending the prayer meeting with Manya wasn't my first experience of this sort. A few years back, I had accompanied the
shoe heiress from Saint Louis to her Manhattan Christian Science
church in gratitude for being cured of a twenty-four-hour intes-
tinal flu in one day. After enjoying an elegant dinner at the Cos-
mopolitan Club with her glamorous mother and the fashionable
woman who had prayed for my healing over the phone, we
crossed Park Avenue to the plush 65th Street church for the

regular Wednesday evening show-and-tell service. There I heard perfectly coifed ladies in minks offer their personal testimonies how God had demonstrated His power; not only by healing their various ailments but by fulfilling their material aspirations, whether finding the right apartment or having their financial investments perform miraculously well. With this kind of personal information being divulged by so many single, rich women, no wonder I spotted in the comfortably upholstered pews a smattering of well-groomed single men in custom tailored suits, distinguished by four handcrafted button holes on each sleeve. While the motives of these confreres may have been questionable, I was there solely to please my Christian Science friend. Thinking I would please her still more, I stood up on a sudden impulse during a lull between testimonies to deliver one of my own. "I'm not a Christian Scientist, but some of my best friends are," I started with appropriate gravity. "And because one of them happened to be with me at a critical moment in the middle of the night, I'm fortunate to have been saved from an unpleasant malady." I launched into a detailed but tactful explanation of my diarrhea, followed by general ruminations about God, life, and the human condition. Never for a moment did I think that anyone in the church might draw untoward conclusions from this testimony about the nature of my relationship with the shoe heiress at my side. But as soon as I sat down, she gave me an angry look. "You bastard, now everybody knows!" she hissed, clearly upset since sex outside of marriage was a fundamental *no no*, or error, among the Christian Science faithful. At the end of the service, however, when several of the older women congratulated me on my inspiring testimony, my intimate partner stood proudly at my side. Even the minister made the unprecedented move of stepping down from the podium to give me a personal pitch for joining the Christian Science Church. However, a few days later my lovely friend was again doing a slow burn. All these years she had been hoping to gather enough courage to give a testimony of her own as a demonstration of her faith. Yet, there I was, a self-proclaimed fornicator who had done it as a lark, and all those old ladies fell for it.

The meeting where Manya had brought me was unlike the Park Avenue church. From a glimpse of the people filling several rows of the brown metal folding chairs in the auditorium of the local parochial school, I realized there would be no minks here, no four buttonholes on each sleeve — and thank God for that. This was the last place I wanted to be seen by any of those compeers. I would find it no less embarrassing than for some of the occupants of these chairs to be caught at an X-rated film. I had too many answers about life to be entrusting myself to some simplistic approach geared to people who seemed to be foundering and in need of help.

Standing on a little podium in front of a provisional altar, Al paused to scan his somber-faced audience. "I know how happy all of you are to be here," said the plumber-turned-preacher with a touch of levity. "I only wish every now and then you'd let your faces know."

I felt the muscles of my jaw momentarily relax before resuming their grim set. Just because I was a sucker for corny jokes didn't mean that Al's observation applied to me. But since I wanted to make my sister happy, I held onto the hymnal with Manya, I mouthed a few of the prayers I knew, and I listened impassively to individual attendees praise Jesus. If only they didn't always get so carried away in calling out to *Gee-zhus!* Some of them sounded as if they were mental patients on furlough, especially the rotund woman a few rows behind us who came forth with a torrent of gibberish, which I presumed was speaking in tongues.

"Appah, appah beezak, tooey hoo karrooh!" I heard her conclude with a flourish.

"Alleluia," responded several people around me, including my sister. "Alleluia."

"What was all that about," I muttered to Manya.

"She's talking directly to God," my sister whispered back. "It's her soul speaking. Only He understands."

I was trying to think of a clever repartee when my attention was distracted by a lithe twenty-year-old sitting in one of the front rows. Maybe there was something to being here after all, if people like her came. My gaze then traveled past her to a small band accompanying the singing of the hymns. Playing the tambourine was a girl with a dwarfish body and a grotesquely large head. She had been born with a pituitary gland tumor that took her sight — at least, that's what my sister whispered to me when she saw me watching this victim of fate's cruelty jiggle and strike her instrument so happily. As my eyes came to rest again and again on this girl's pitiful form, her cheerful radiance made me realize how little cause I had for gloom.

"Praise be . . ." somebody called out. Then from another part of the room, "Praise be, oh sweet Jesus!"

I tried to force my mouth into position so that I, too, could hurl forth expletives of praise. Yet even though my lips moved, no sound emerged. It would have made Manya so happy, especially if I could do it with that same Gee-zhus verve. What was embarrassing me was not just being here among so many self-avowed losers. Had I come as a curious outsider, I could have put on a creditable show. But instead, I was feeling uncomfortably close to being a participant; in fact, needing to be a participant.

"Let us pray," I heard Al, the group leader, intone. He paused to give everyone a chance to stand. "Our all-merciful Lord, put your loving arms around us. Heal us of the hurts we have suffered, forgive us for the sins we have committed . . . forgive us for whatever pain we may have caused others . . . for whatever we did that was wrong . . . for whatever we didn't do that we should have done."

The words continued to flow. I was no longer conscious of Al's brogue, which had a pacifying lilt. I was appreciating his low-key delivery and pauses, which let me think how his words might apply to me. I found it relaxing to close my eyes. I felt a certain comfort, a certain relief from the pressing nature of my cares.

"Thank you, Jesus . . ." Al was concluding, his eyes shut, his voice a whisper. "Thank you for guiding us and protecting us. Thank you for loving us. Thank you for being always there when we needed you the most."

"Thank you, Jesus," somebody interjected.

"Alleluia, Gee-zhus!" another voice chimed in.

As I watched Al link hands with the worshippers standing on either side of him, I felt one hand gently grasped by my sister and the other by a white-haired woman on the other side of me.

I felt my arms lifted upward, a crescendo of voices chanting in unison, "Praise be Jesus! Praise be! Praise be! Praise be Jesus our Lord!"

Once more, Al took the lead. "Oh Lord Jesus, hear our prayer. We ask for this moment of silence to bring before you our special requests. We entrust to you our most private thoughts so that thy will be done, and our burdens will be lighter to bear."

There was an extended pause. My eyes were pressed shut, and I was welcoming this moment of peace. It was like those five-second silent prayers I had continued to offer since childhood under various circumstances to whoever was in charge in the yonder world: *Please God, keep me safe and sound, protect my parents whom I love, and spare me any personal calamities such as breaking an arm or a leg in St. Moritz, or God forbid, cause an unwanted pregnancy or pick up and pass on some intimate disease.* Now, as I was about to run through a more pertinent version of this litany, I experienced an overwhelming surprise. Before I was able to make a single wish, I sensed a distinct but seamless shift, as if someone had gently turned a rheostatic switch. I felt a soothing, all-pervasive light illuminate the darkness within my brain and banish the somberness lurking there. I was filled with a light-headedness, a liberation from worldly cares, and a sense of unabashed gratitude for this radiant moment. Any notion of embarrassment as to where I was and what I was doing here had disappeared. I couldn't think of a problem I had or a request I wanted to make. All I could feel was a sense of inner strength, inner warmth, inner peace which couldn't be shaken. It was so sudden, so total that I couldn't question it or compare it to anything else. For the first time in my life I felt as if I needed nothing else. Oh, it felt so comforting and good. Oh, how thankful I was! Yes, thank you, thank you, thank you, Jesus.

The meeting was over. Around me people were embracing in that special, communal way. I released the hand of the old woman next to me and turned to look directly at her for the first time. She smiled, put her arms around me, and whispered, "Welcome back."

I didn't realize I had been that obvious. But I didn't mind. I was suffused by an outgoing warmth reinforcing the profound gratitude I was continuing to feel.

My sister also noticed the change. We didn't embrace since Manya had always been restrained about any show of physicality. But her eyes were shining and proud. I was her pupil whom she had been able to make see the light. All those prayers, all those persistent efforts I had spurned or ridiculed, had come to fruition before her eyes. It was proof that Jesus was real, that he was doing his work among us to this day. What greater miracle could anyone imagine than to witness what was happening to me just then?

With proprietary pride, Manya introduced me to several women who came by to say hello. They gave each other knowing looks, as if they were familiar with my case and had been praying on my behalf.

I didn't mind this public exposure. My lightheadedness verged on giddiness, and that nagging restlessness, which had been making me teary eyed, had vanished. I was free and without a problem. In my exuberance, I edged over to the attractive young woman I had been watching earlier, and we began to chat with a natural spontaneity. I felt the same loving communion toward her as I did when chatting with that elderly woman and my sister's other friends, who now seemed to be endowed with the same human worth. She told me she had come with her fiancé, a regular member of the group. This was her first time, too.

"You coming again?" I asked.

She glanced at her escort, and then nodded with a smile. "I suppose so."

"It kind of grows on you," I said, as if I were an old regular. "Maybe I'll see you around."

On the way back to my sister's house, my elation didn't abate.

"It's called being slain in the spirit," Manya explained. She recounted how it had happened to her years ago when her marriage was collapsing and she was in desperate straits. "I know how you feel," she concluded. "It put me on cloud nine, too."

We talked with a closeness we had never experienced before. There was a sense of being partners in something grand yet intensely personal, as we both bubbled over with unrestrained joy. Our sharing of happiness was akin to two people reverting to reality after making love for the first time and glimpsing a fantastic new dimension that promised to fill their lives with bliss. Feeling this way with my sister seemed almost indecent.

"So Jesus got to you, too," Manya's husband greeted us with good-natured humor on returning home. He wanted to have peace in the family and, over the years, accommodated my sister to the point of accompanying her to charismatic weekend retreats. "You don't know how happy you've made Manya. She's been praying for this, God only knows how long. As a matter of fact, she said a prayer for you today just before you came."

"Would you please keep quiet," Manya protested mildly.

"I might even get a little loving tonight," he said jovially, "thanks to you and Jesus."

My sister's nervous laugh reflected her embarrassment. "Not if you talk this way, you won't."

After bidding my hosts an especially cordial goodnight, I went upstairs to the guest room. I undressed, opened the window, and slid under the covers before the cold air could trail me in. But I wasn't about to fall asleep. I still felt as if I were riding one of those oxygen highs I had experienced on returning from a week of skiing in the Alps, with extra red blood cells coursing through

31

my veins. I knew this could be a crucial point in my life. I had always suspected, in the back of my mind, that sooner or later I would return to religion. Probably later, much later; perhaps like my old friend Fuzzy Sedgwick, who had been a great bon vivant and philanderer until practically his next-to-last breath, despite a loving wife and a brood of children and grandchildren. But being also an avid historian, he had asked on his deathbed to be converted to the Roman Catholic faith just in case there was something to it in view of its unique two-thousand-year unbroken tradition. Certainly, no harm in touching all bases! Yes, I too had expected eventually to crawl back into the fold to play it safe. But never, never did I suspect I would accept Christ honestly, with no reservations, under no extreme duress. Thank you, Jesus, thank you for sparing me from having to be a hypocrite in my final moments on earth.

I lay there in bed in an alert trance. Rushing through my head, I could feel the miraculous truth of Christ continuing to reveal itself. I could for the first time understand the unique opportunity inherent in bringing Christ into every aspect of my life. Through Jesus Christ our Lord . . . what a meaning in those words! No wonder my relationship with Katherine had failed. How difficult it was to do anything without Jesus, yet how easy when you let him carry part of the load. What a sustaining force!

Absorbing the warmth of my bed, I felt euphoric over this insight, which went beyond anything I had previously intuited or learned. How exciting to think of all the people I would be able to influence in this powerful new way! When it came to advising others on key issues in life, I enjoyed an implicit credibility among a wide circle of friends. What a heady feeling to think of the lives I would now be able to change in this incomparably more important way! *Thank you, Jesus; so this was your plan for me all along!* Indeed, I might become famous using my public relations savvy to serve a worthy goal. What an unparalleled perspective I had, having been on the other side, one of the misguided for so many years. I would be able to show others how to take away the burdens of daily life . . . how much better they can live when everything is no longer of ultimate import . . . when there's something so much greater . . . when there's Jesus Christ.

Oh God! I was exulting to myself. *All my life I wanted to know what my role was. I was close for so long, yet I couldn't see it. I thought I was free before . . . but I was such a slave! Now I know . . . it's the scales falling from my eyes. If I've flipped, please let me stay flipped. Oh Jesus, don't ever go away from me . . . or withdraw from my life!*

I could hear the wind blowing outside, sending gusts of frigid air through the open window. I felt so warm and secure under the blankets, protected and looking forward to tomorrow morning, to starting my new life.

Is this what was meant *to be born again* – or as I would later learn was a more accurate translation, *to be reborn from above?*

When I awoke, I didn't want to face myself. I pulled the pillow over my head, trying to shut out the reality of the previous night. While I had none of the physical symptoms of a hangover, I felt as if I were coming out of a terrible drunk. I had slobbered all over myself with words, committed emotional excesses, and succumbed to embarrassing indiscretions of the mind. On top of that, I was again beginning to experience that strange, restless feeling I thought had left me for good.

How could I have allowed my judgment to become so impaired? I felt myself cringe within, remembering those extravagant details I had spewed forth about Jesus, about my new life in Christ and converting the world on his behalf. Hadn't my experience really been a case of autosuggestion, a form of self-hypnosis? I had seen people turned on with equal rapture by Maharai Ji, the Reverend Moon, the Hare Krishnas, Tim Leary, Baba Ram Das, and a variety of other gurus and prophets of our time.

Fortunately, the only person I had to face was my sister, and I hadn't been nearly as effusive with her as in my thoughts.

Manya was awaiting me in the kitchen. "How *are* you?" she asked probingly, as she finished squeezing my juice of two oranges and a grapefruit. I could see in her expression the same joy she had shared with me the previous night, but which I could no longer reciprocate.

"I slept just fine," I said, deliberately noncommittal. "The bed in that room is really comfortable."

An uneasy silence ensued while she hovered over the stove and then served me my soft-boiled eggs. I knew what she was thinking: After working on me all those years, had she lost me so soon?

She was delighted when I asked for another piece of toast, and would she mind making some coffee after all? "I could really use a lift," I explained.

This seemed to be the opening Manya was waiting for. "I think I know how you feel," she started cautiously. "You shouldn't let it worry you if you're a little down today. That's not at all unusual."

"Now you tell me," I said, trying to keep it light. "Is there an antidote?"

Manya was measuring out the ground coffee for the percolator and paused to give me a reassuring look. "What you must do is trust the Lord. Don't be afraid. Trust the Lord."

I tried not to betray an instant of exasperation. It was this kind of an answer that had led me to conclude in recent years that my sister was compromising her intelligence.

"Anything else?" I asked.

"You must pray. Whenever you can, you must pray and read the Bible. That's the way the Lord will speak to you."

"So that's what those priests and little old nuns are doing when I see them with their open Bibles on buses and trains! I always wondered what was the point of reading the same stuff over and over again."

"It's the only way to overcome your doubts and become strong in your faith."

"Sounds like brainwashing to me."

Manya glanced at me uneasily, as if I were blaspheming. "It's a great gift. I hope you take advantage of it." She brought me the toast and remained standing by my chair. "To pray, to read the word of the Lord . . . in fact, anything he inspired others to write . . . whether saints, humble priests, or everyday people."

"And I suppose," I interjected a bit sarcastically, "I should also go to meetings and all that."

"By all means. As often as possible."

"But you always made it sound like a one-shot deal. I thought all I had to do was come to *a* meeting."

"I certainly didn't mean it that way. Don't you see, it's a commitment for a lifetime. There's no going back."

I crunched on my remaining piece of toast. "You sound like Dr. Bieler."

"Dr. Bieler?"

"An old medical doctor in California who also claimed there was no going back if I wanted to be saved. Two raw egg yolks and steamed zucchini for breakfast as long as I lived . . . if I

35

wanted to live. Yet, look at me, here I am, almost ten years later, enjoying every strictly verboten item, even the toast and orange juice weren't allowed. Doesn't that tell you something?"

My sister looked bewildered. "How can you compare the two!"

"Don't forget, Jesus was known primarily as a healer in his time. Making the blind see, casting out evil spirits . . ."

"That's different. Those were miracles."

"In many parts of the world, tribal priests still double as doctors. They know the importance of keeping body and soul together."

Manya seemed embarrassed for my sake. "But that's witchcraft. They're pagans. Just remember, Jesus loves you."

"Why can't I distill out of this Jesus stuff what's right for me . . . the way I did out of all that Bieler rigmarole?"

"Don't you see, you can't do it alone? None of us can do it alone." Manya paused to give me a telling look. "Besides, it's a mortal sin if you don't go to church."

The last phrase instantly made my dander rise. Obviously, she meant the Catholic Church; that authoritarian hierarchy with its spiteful internal politics and the nasty habit of arrogating to itself a monopoly of truth. Back in my intellectual history class at Yale, Professor Baumer alerted us to the perils of such a fallacious mindset. The evidence was certainly there, reflected in the horrors committed in Christ's name, whether the merciless slaughter perpetrated during the Crusades, the unimaginable tortures inflicted by the Inquisition, or the suppression of ideas to this day. If there indeed was any validity to my experience the previous night – to that liberating infusion of light which supposedly had been the visitation of Christ – I would stay open to exploring it on my own. But damn if I would do it through the Church! I hadn't been in thirty years, and I wasn't about to go

she must have suffered to have almost turned on the gas! How many of my former loves would have been better off had they never become involved with me? The statuesque stockbroker, Annette, whom I had met the previous year while strolling along Fifth Avenue, had been right in calling me a fraud. Seething with anger as she ended our brief affair, she fired off her salvo: I really ought to carry a sandwich board, strapped over one of my custom-made suits as if advertising somebody's eatery, spelling out the truth: I didn't have a proper place to live, lacked a reliable job, and certainly harbored no marriage intentions.

God certainly needed no such sandwich board to see through me now! YES, YOU HAVE SINNED . . .

Standing there as if stuck to the frozen snow, I felt stripped bare, fully exposed by this scroll of wrongs unraveling from a past I had rarely examined or recalled. I was now being forced to see how I had misused my life. I had received so much, including a privileged education with the expectation that I would use the knowledge to help others and make the world a better place. Before me now was the scowling, fatherly face the Duke, my old headmaster who had granted me nearly a full scholarship and ensured I also received one at Yale, where he had been an esteemed trustee. Indeed, I had often told myself while working as world affairs editor at Scholastic Magazines, or promoting student travel programs at the American Institute for Foreign Study, and then helping publicize the global outreach of the Peace Corps in Washington, that I was fulfilling the Duke's expectations by contributing to international understanding and good will. Yet how clearly I now recognized that my primary goal had been to make the world as comfortable for myself as I could, even at the cost of twisting or otherwise compromising the truth. An array of episodes flashed through my mind,

41

highlighted by the agonized features of the editor-in-chief at *Family Weekly*, wishing he could throw out the eight-million printing run of a promotional article on the Institute I had foisted on him as a public service by implying it was a non-profit company. No amount of sophistry or rationalization could make me look one iota better than I was being shown to be. My frivolous attitude about life, which people had often found so charming and quaint, was being exposed as one continuous sin. How proud I had been of the sparkling beaches I had once enjoyed, the spectacular mountains I had skied, the vintage wines and delectable foods I had savored, the exotic women with whom I had partnered, the wonderful places I had visited around the globe, even congratulating myself for having experienced a thousand times the pleasures allotted to a normal life. Now, to my distress, I was being called to account for it all.

BY WHAT RIGHT DID YOU DO THOSE THINGS? SOMEBODY ELSE HAD TO SACRIFICE AND STRUGGLE MIGHTILY TO MAKE POSSIBLE YOUR INDULGENT LIFE. AND HOW ABOUT THOSE THIN-FACED MILLIONS WHO AT THIS MOMENT LACK THE NECESSITIES OF LIFE WHILE YOU ARE HAVING MANY TIMES YOUR SHARE? WHAT MADE YOU THINK YOU COULD HAVE TWO ORANGES AND A PINK GRAPEFRUIT FOR BREAKFAST EACH DAY, WHEN EMACIATED CHILDREN ALL OVER THE WORLD ARE DYING FOR LACK OF A SINGLE WEDGE?

Hoping to disrupt this distressing link, I ducked into the woods. I could barely make out the darkening sky through the heavy branches of the tall evergreens, but the messages continued to bombard me without a pause. BY WHAT REASONING DID YOU THINK THAT ONE DAY YOU WOULDN'T BE HANDED A BILL? My sudden awareness of its staggering size was making me wobble at the knees. No wonder the more luxurious stores discreetly hid the price tags on their most expensive goods! Only it was too late for me to suspend my shopping spree and slink away.

Desperately I searched for something with which I might be able to pay at least in part. I tried to recall the good deeds I had done, the sacrifices I had made, the occasions I had inconvenienced myself to do what was right. Oh sure, during my first Navy cruise, I had placed a bundle of discarded clothes in front of a refugee hovel in Hong Kong, before picking up my new suits at Mohan's custom tailors. More recently, I sent a fifty-dollar check to the Biafra hunger fund. I invariably gave handouts to derelicts in the streets and occasionally stopped for hitchhikers in the rain. But all of that added up to a paltry sum that made no difference on the bill. I was a beggar at Tiffany's, trying to pay off an overdue invoice with pennies in my hand.

INDEED, THERE WILL BE A PRICE TO PAY . . .

Surrounded by the pine-scented woods, I felt queasy from the relentless onslaught. Yet I now found myself having to contend also with a message of a different sort. I was beginning to see myself as a cassock-clad priest, praying on my knees and impervious in body and mind to anything impure. This new tableau puzzled me until it dawned on me: Is this what it felt like to be called? I had always considered the tales of receiving God's call and grappling with it as self-delusions of Catholic young men afraid of life, and especially, sex. Yet that's what seemed to be happening to me now; yes, that was it, the only way to make amends was to become one of those porcine celibates. Oh, what a grotesque twist of fate! The thought constricted me within, tightening its painful grip around my churning innards and adding another dimension to my internal stress.

God, how screwed up could I be! I reflected. Lucky there was no mirror to see how terribly pale I must have turned, the last of my Florida tan neutralized. Maybe the best thing was to cut short my walk, go home, and make myself a good meal. Mother had bought me an excellent veal chop, which I would enhance with a superb bottle of 1969 Saint Estèphe. Maybe that would infuse my brain with some sense and clarify my muddled thoughts! I normally drank only half a bottle at a time, but I might want to make an exception today. A vintage Bordeaux such as this didn't keep well once uncorked, and it would be a sin to let it spoil.

Feeling myself grimace at this unwitting rationale, I called out into the darkness of the woods, "C'mon, Blackie, we're going home."

5/

I hadn't eaten since breakfast. Despite abbreviating that distressing walk and returning early, I started making dinner right away. Mother usually fixed Sunday lunch, but the rest of the time I was on my own. I was especially glad she wasn't hovering near me now. She would know right away I was in some unspeakable fix. And what could I say? She was a practical person who shared my religious apathy and had little patience for the fairy tales preached in church. Embarrassed that Manya had become a born again Jesus devotee (unlike my younger sister Eve), Mother made her promise not to proselytize at the Christmas gatherings of our extended family. How could I now tell Mother that God had personally rebuked me a few minutes ago and was ordering that I become a priest?

I turned the oven to broil, determined to concentrate on the culinary task and forget, at least for now, what I had been through at the edge of the woods. I opened the refrigerator to take out the meat and place it on a cutting board. Good veal was difficult to find. I still remembered the veal chop prepared by a chef in Italy at a hilltop restaurant over the Tyrrhenian Sea. I had sent back his first offering with precise criticism: The meat was from an inferior cut and leathery, and the pasta tasted stiff, about fifty-five seconds underdone. The chef must have realized I wasn't another tourist to be dispatched with scorn. He personally brought out his next attempt, a huge loin that looked juicy on the serving tray, and then stood by with pride as he waited for me to take the first bite. Of course, I deluged him with praise, which made him beam, as did the tip I bestowed on him afterwards when I went to the kitchen to thank him.

The chop for tonight promised to be just as good. I could practically savor it already cooked, along with the yellow wax beans and the thin capellini spaghetti topped with melted butter and freshly grated Parmesan cheese. This would be preceded by a Bieler-sized green salad, deviating radically from the old doctor's no-dressing proscription with my own creation, concocted from vinegar, Maître Jacques Dijon mustard, olive oil, and a sprinkling of crumbled Gorgonzola cheese. But what would truly make the meal was the bottle of ten-year-old Saint Estèphe, the last of a half-case I had discovered at the local package store.

I pulled the cork, sniffed it, and set it aside. I carefully poured a small amount of the wine into a large goblet of very thin glass. I swirled it around and brought it to my nose. Uhmm . . . how well the wine would go with the meal . . . especially the tannin which would balance the richness in the spaghetti and the meat. This was the sort of combination that might snap me back to life.

By now I had the chop laid out on aluminum foil, with dabs of butter and a little rosemary on top. It was time to turn on the burners under the beans and the water for the spaghetti. The veal I would put in the oven when the beans began to boil, and the thin capellini spaghetti would go in the boiling water last.

That way everything would be done at about the same time — the secret of fine cuisine. In the meantime, I would sip from my exquisite glass, which held almost enough for the entire meal. The uncorked wine's continued exposure to air would further enhance its bouquet.

I filled the glass and raised it for what was to be the first real sip. Uhmm, that dark ruby red Saint Estèphe . . . how it would mellow the brain and help me forget those messages for good!

The glass never reached my lips. With the force of an unexpected blow, I felt an implacable command coming through in non-negotiable terms: NO DINNER TONIGHT. THAT'S RIGHT, NO DINNER FOR YOU TONIGHT!

Incredulous, I shook my head. It was as if some deep-seated organic pain had just stabbed me anew. I couldn't believe this was happening to me here in the protective warmth of the kitchen at my parents' home.

I glanced around, wine glass poised at my lips. I mustn't give in! I have to fight this crazy thing. Just a few inches and then tilt a bit, and I shall be having a sip.

NO, AND AGAIN, NO! That wordless message seemed to reverberate within my brain like an echo between a range of towering peaks. NO DINNER MEANS NO WINE. YOU'VE GOT A HEAVY PRICE TO PAY . . . AND YOU ARE GOING TO START PAYING IT NOW!

It was a command that made the fear of the Almighty distressingly real.

I put aside the glass and slowly sat down. God, what was happening to me?

As I glanced toward the stove, the threat of no dinner intensified my hunger pangs. Seeing the water under the beans begin to boil, I realized it was time to start cooking the veal.

I stood up and opened the oven, turning my face away from the hot blast of air. The temperature felt about right. I took a step toward the cutting board and reached to pick up the veal on the aluminum foil.

This time, the message came through with the intensity of a storm: YOU HEARD, NO DINNER TONIGHT. TURN OFF THOSE FLAMES AND PUT AWAY THE FOOD!

Petrified, I stood there holding the uncooked veal. Was this an ominous beginning to a pattern that would twist and tangle my life into an agonizing mess? Was this how Joan of Arc had heard and heeded her voices — and ended up being burned at the stake?

For a few seconds I walked around the stove, abjectly miserable yet not daring to disobey. Acting as if in a trance, I put the veal back on the cutting board and turned off the stove. First the broiler, then the two burners on top. The water for the spaghetti I poured out next. Moving like an automaton and trying not to think, I drained off the yellow beans, wrapped the chop in aluminum foil, and corked up the wine. I hadn't felt this kind of emptiness in my stomach since the day I embarked on Dr. Bieler's draconian regimen. But that was necessary then. I had to recover from starch toxemia, or whatever I had. God, what in the world did I have now?

Dejected to the extreme, I opened the refrigerator door and started to put everything away, already imagining the long, empty evening ahead.

As I was about to finish that task, I suddenly felt another message coming through. And right away, I could tell it was different in tone: OKAY, YOU PASSED, YOU CAN HAVE YOUR DINNER NOW. BUT WE SHALL BE TALKING AGAIN . . . SOON.

This was crazy! Nevertheless, I felt sufficiently relieved to start taking everything out of the refrigerator again. But what did it all mean? Especially this talking again soon? What surprise did I have to steel myself for next? Was this what it meant to go out of your mind? Surely, that's what an impartial observer would have to conclude from the way I was behaving in the kitchen, turning on the stove and redoing everything I had undone only moments before. Yet I knew how terribly sane I felt, how overly rational – which is what was scaring me the most.

This disconcerted state of mind didn't keep me from enjoying the meal. The wine tasted even more delicious than I remembered, though alas, it didn't brighten my mood. Would I ever find peace again, I wondered, as I finished off the last of the capellini and veal. How relatively predictable and straightforward my life used to be! What would Manya say about this inexplicable turn of events? Would she have some comforting words? Trust the Lord, she had said, pray to him and read his word . . . and whatever he inspired others to write.

I raised my glass for another prolonged sip; suddenly as if on cue, I had a fortuitous thought that made me bolt from the kitchen to the living room. What I remembered was that over the past ten years my sister had been bombarding every member of the family with a barrage of religious books. Most were simplistic, not much beyond the level of pulp fiction. But others were by writers I had studied in Baumer's intellectual history class – Saint Augustine, Thomas à Kempis, Thomas Aquinas and the like. If I managed to find one of those, perhaps the answer would become clear.

We didn't have a library, but in the living room was a long, Renaissance table from our palace in Prague (one of the few antiques Father had managed to whisk out in time) where he now did his paperwork. Here stacks of books were haphazardly piled along with an accumulation of Exercycle invoices and bills, back copies of various health magazines, and political monographs from obscure Central European émigré groups. More of the same was piled along every window ledge as well as on the mantle over the large stone fireplace. Father favored biographies of powerful contemporaries, chronicles of World War II, and spy thrillers. Still, if I rummaged long enough through this assorted mess, I might find one of Manya's books that had somehow missed being thrown out.

I went to the first pile, intending to go through it book by book, then repeat the procedure with other piles. But I was startled by what happened next. The very first book I picked up had on its cover a prominent white cross and was titled *The Seven Storey Mountain* by someone called Thomas Merton. I glanced at the publisher's blurb: "The extraordinary autobiography that has become a modern spiritual classic – the testament of an intensely active and brilliant young man who decided to withdraw from the world only after he had fully immersed himself in it."

I shuddered. Even if I hardly considered myself a *brilliant* young man, could that part about withdrawing from the world after fully immersing himself in it apply to me? Merely coming across this work seemed eerily more than coincidental.

Merton's book in hand, I returned to the kitchen to clear the table and stack the dishes in the sink. As I was corking up what remained of the wine, I noted with momentary satisfaction that the bottle was still better than half-full. Why not take the Saint Estèphe up to my room? It might be just what I needed to accompany Merton's book and make his message go down more easily.

I glanced once more at the stove to make sure the burners were off. I tucked the promising tome under one arm and started to pick up the bottle and glass.

NOT SO FAST . . . I felt that implacable command stop me in my tracks. FIRST, POUR OUT THAT WINE!

I found myself struggling to reason. *Think of the labor that went into this vintage, think of the years it took to produce it. And to waste it all now?*

IN THE SINK!

If I leave it in the fridge, it'll keep . . .

IN THE SINK! It was a thunderous command that brooked no delay. Putting down the glass and Merton's book, I inverted the bottle and mournfully watched the tempting liquid hurtle out and disappear down the drain.

From behind my back I heard, "What are you doing that for?" It was Mother's voice. She had come into the kitchen in time to see me empty the last of the wine.

I resisted the impulse to face her. "I'm afraid this bottle has turned," I mumbled over the sink. Then, sensing Mother still there, I started to fidget with the dishes.

"Never mind those," she said. "I'll take care of them . . . as I always do."

"I think I'll go up to read and turn in early." I tried to sneak past Mother, thinking how ridiculous for a man in his mid-forties to be afraid of being found out.

She stepped in front of me. "Are you all right?"

I paused but didn't look up. "I guess I'm a bit tired."

She sized me up with a worried look. I could tell by her wrinkled brow that she sensed I was somehow unwell in a different way. "I never believed my mother's warning that only after children grew up would they really cause you grief," Mother sighed, then gave me a sharp glance. "I hope you aren't coming down with something. Don't expect me to take care of you."

I managed to squeeze out a smile. I knew Mother would enjoy nothing more than taking care of me, provided, of course, it wasn't serious.

"By the way, Manya sends her love," I remarked offhandedly, giving in to Mother's gaze. I didn't want to cause my sister difficulties over her proselytizing zeal. But when Mother continued to gaze at me expectantly, I felt compelled to add, "She took me to one of her meetings."

"I knew it, she's been working on you again!"

"I went because I wanted to."

"You?"

"Well, I've been thinking during the last few days . . . I'm really not a good person."

"Nonsense," Mother said with a unusual firmness. Despite her docile exterior she held in reserve a steely determination she would employ when necessary. "You've always been kind and generous. Everybody says that about you."

"You yourself often said I had a skewed outlook on life."

"It's my fault we hadn't been strict enough in bringing you up."

"I've also been self-centered."

"Just like your father." Mother furrowed her brow, a habitual expression acquired years ago over Father's irremediable roving eye. "You inherited that."

"Except that Father always came through when it counted."

"He's not like other people," Mother said, and made a quick, dismissive wave of her arm. "You're merely complaining about being normal."

"That's how I always tried to rationalize it, too. Unfortunately, it doesn't work anymore."

Mother flashed me a look of anger. "What in the world did Manya do to you?"

"Please, don't blame her. Whatever is going to happen isn't her fault."

"And what is going to happen?"

I shrugged and made a grimace, then went upstairs with the Merton book.

6/

I was glad to be in my room, which felt cozy and warm. The closed window was already covered with the intricate designs of frost, and the occasional rattle from the radiator had the reassuring effect of a crackling fire. Though it wasn't quite seven, I would do my reading in bed. I was feeling as if I were somehow ill. Was I perhaps undergoing the spiritual version of Dr. Bieler's surgery without knives, whereby the poisons accumulated in the body's tissues by years of physical excesses were purged through his rigid regimen? Did the long-term moral poisons I had accumulated over the years and kept carefully hidden in the back of my mind suddenly start pouring out in the form of that agonizing reckoning on the snowy field?

Shaking off this disturbing notion, I undressed and put on my winter sleeping attire, an old cashmere turtleneck with multiple holes that made it unsuitable for anything else. I spread out my worn-out sheepskin coat over the lower part of the bed, then fluffed the two pillows to prop up my back.

I was beginning to feel better. Surely, the crazy internal compulsions I had been experiencing would disappear, along with those irrational religious thoughts, and I would be able to reaffirm who I was. While my symptoms seemed strange, this sort of thing undoubtedly happened every day, especially to men around my age. If I were to seek psychiatric help, my case would most likely be viewed as nothing out of the ordinary.

I turned on the little lamp at the side of my bed and flicked off the overhead light. Then I opened Merton's book.

The very first paragraph riveted my attention: "I came into this world . . . the prisoner of my own violence and my own selfishness, in the image of the world into which I was born. That world was the picture of hell, full of men like myself, loving God and yet hating him; born to love him, living instead in fear and hopeless, self-contradictory hunger."

I had come across such sentences in Professor Baumer's class, and occasionally in other courses too. It was the kind of material I had studied in the abstract, so that I could draw appropriate comparisons between different modes of thought and do well in my hour tests. But as far as I was personally concerned, it added up to so many empty words, unrelated to anything I had experienced in life. More than once, I had disparaged such ideas as intellectual chaff.

Now, I found myself reading from a startlingly different perspective; from a perspective that was my life, and at a critical juncture at that. As I continued down the page and then further into Merton's book, his words not only spoke to me, just as my sister had predicted, but seemed specifically written to be seen by me at this particular moment in my life. Here was a worldly writer searching for an elusive goal, which had held him back from making a commitment either to a profession or a wife. Perhaps that was the reason for my own lack of commitment, as I had fleetingly recognized during my exuberant night at Manya's.

Some of the lesser details of Merton's life also meshed to a remarkable degree with mine, though I did conclude that he had most likely never engaged in sex, perhaps not even in heavy necking. If the sexual revolution I had enjoyed came a generation too late for Merton's youth, I doubted he would have indulged had he been a contemporary of mine.

Merton's absorbing style continued to draw me in. Even without the half-bottle of wine, I was recovering my aplomb. Surely Merton would indicate a way out of my dilemma.

As he began to detail his disillusionment with life and search for new pathways and goals, I was no less eager to tag along. Alas, too late did I realize that the road he was traveling led to prayerful submission to God — precisely where I didn't want to go. Merton's graphic descriptions of his all-night vigils left me queasy and shocked. I had stayed up only two nights in my life, while serving as a young naval officer in the South China Sea. That had been an exciting time, as we steamed in formation with a dozen ships, refueling underway at fifteen knots, a destroyer to starboard and a carrier to port, while Filipino stewards brought hot coffee and scrambled eggs to the moonlit bridge. But praying all night? I had never prayed more than a few seconds at a time, even under the most favorable conditions. I shuddered at the thought of doing so for three, six, perhaps eight hours without a break; kneeling on a wooden bench in an unheated chapel, hands cold from the night's penetrating chill, fighting sleep and the urgent temptation to let my rear sag against my heels. The sole relief would come from clutching a rosary ever more intently and repeating my prayerful words ever more fervently; and after this seemingly endless ordeal, breakfasting on a bowl of tepid gruel, then returning to a dank cell-like room and not finding any warmth under the scratchy, thin blanket covering a hard pallet.

Yet that would be just another typical night of the rest of my life.

I groaned as I set aside Merton's book. I had never experienced such an adverse reaction from reading mere words. No wonder this book was making my illness worse! It was as if I had tried to put my mind at ease before heavy surgery by reading the most grisly descriptions of how they would cut me up and what agonies I would have to endure. Merton had sought to present a most disagreeable experience as near orgasmic joy. He must have been a secret masochist. No, no, I wasn't like him after all.

Yet even as I sought to distance myself from this Cistercian monk, I was beginning to be possessed by another dimension of his life. I was coming to sense what it would be like to become celibate; not just to withdraw from engaging in sex for practical reasons for a given period of time, but to resort actively and deliberately to the permanent suppression of this elemental drive and become a different human being, with different thoughts, different smells, different movements and expressions. I could feel myself being enshrouded in long clerical robes that would protect my lower body from the sensuality of this world and help me be vigilant against any dangerous thoughts.

God, what if Katherine could see me in this state! I glanced at the little photo of her propped up on my dresser. I had taken it when our relationship was already starting to turn but before she gave up hope. I could see the hurt in her eyes, yet the consuming physicality still evident in her expression brought back a poignant scene. I had fallen asleep prematurely after too much champagne and a few drags on an overpowering joint, and awoke some hours later to find Katherine watching me mournfully. I couldn't at first get her to tell me what had upset her so. She hemmed and hawed about how distant and uncommunicative I was after smoking grass, how alone she felt with me asleep, how forlorn. Then she blurted it out: I had conked out after only ten minutes of making love. She sounded reproachful and hurt, as if I had inflicted on her a grievous wound.

Now glancing at Katherine's photo once more, I again noticed in her eyes an overpowering sensuality, which made me cower and withdraw further into my celibate mood.

It wasn't nine o'clock yet, but I would try to fall asleep. I quickly got out of bed to open the window, then jumped back in on a bound to outrace the blast of frigid air. I flipped off the table light and pulled the covers tightly around me, leaving only my head exposed. The cold against my face made me all the more aware of the secure warmth of my bed.

For a moment I lay there, trying to make my mind go blank. In the next moment, I was on my knees, as if compelled from within, muttering, *Oh, please God, give me the sense to make heads or tails of this mess. You've always helped make things turn out right. How about doing it for me again just this once?*

That ought to do it, I thought to myself as if to say, *Amen.* Nevertheless, I remained kneeling ramrod straight. I could feel the protective layer of warmth being absorbed by the frigid air streaming in, and I was beginning to shiver. Is this what it felt like for Merton during his all-night vigils? Secure in the knowledge I could dart back under the covers whenever I chose, I remained kneeling a few seconds more to get a still more vivid idea of those sleepless vigils in the cold.

7/

My condition failed to improve over the next couple of days. I hadn't received any more of those unwelcome messages. But I slept fitfully both nights, finding myself frequently on my knees, praying with unrestrained fervor for help.

My sister was right. These sporadic bursts of devotion did bring momentary relief. But I wasn't about to call Manya for more of her well-meaning advice. That's how I had ended up with Merton's *Seven Storey Mountain*. No wonder books like his left me unmoved in the past! The mind had to be appropriately pre-disposed and sick before these abnormal exhortations could strike a responsive nerve.

Then on Sunday morning, things got worse. Distraught and consummately sad, as if something of immense value was about to be taken away, I found myself in the throes of a compulsion to go to church. Unlike the previous commands, which seemed to have originated in the beyond, this one felt like a self-gener-ated apprehension about what might happen if I didn't go, per-haps a sort of post-hypnotic suggestion from Manya that I would be committing a mortal sin.

I was embarrassed by what was happening to me and didn't want to worry my parents in any way. Not so much Father; he was too absorbed enjoying himself to notice anything odd over the last couple of days. But Mother had already wondered aloud why I had skipped my usual dinnertime wine twice in a row. She often complained of having to be extra careful in washing my large goblet of thin glass; now, she missed that chore. If I told her I was on my way to church, she would know that only the most compelling personal distress could prompt me to such a drastic move.

As the internal pressure continued to mount, I felt I had no choice but to comply. Even if going to church wouldn't bring me the relief I sought, it might help propitiate the angry powers beyond. How well I was beginning to understand why worship was such a time-tested palliative against divine wrath!

Hoping to avoid any fuss, my plan was to slip out quietly. But as I stood up and started to put on my jacket, Mother intervened. "Where're you going?" I heard her voice from her favorite chair in the far end of the living room. "You haven't finished the Sunday paper yet."

"Do I have to tell you everything?" I said peevishly. "I'm no longer eight years old."

Father looked up from the book review section he was reading on the couch. "To Mother, you'll always be about eight years old," he observed with a laugh.

I was already regretting having snapped at Mother. Mustering whatever equanimity I could, I tried to make light of my intent. "I thought I'd go to church and nullify my sins with a prayer or two."

Mother looked distressed. "It was your visit to Manya, I knew it!"

"She had nothing to do with it."

"What I don't understand," Mother continued, "is how someone as intelligent as you could let yourself be influenced by Manya. I was always afraid she might confuse the grandchildren when they came for Christmas. I never imagined it would be you."

"You've always laughed at Manya's devotion," Father reminded me, without looking up from his reading. "Poor girl, she takes it a little too seriously."

Though vastly differing in their respective rationales, Father shared Mother's apathy for the Church. As a teenager in a private Catholic gymnasium in Austria, he had been caught reading Emil Zola and was given a choice to blatantly lie or be kicked out, a deceitful ploy he would never forget. As for Mother, she had inherited her view that the Catholic Church had traditionally sided with the Austro-Hungarian nobility in exploiting shopkeepers such as her family's. (Even though the nobleman she married was known for his notoriously progressive views, Mother never did quite get over this conviction.) Despite my parents' passivity about the Church, the reason both of my sisters started their education in Catholic schools was because girls from titled families had been traditionally *sent to the nuns*, in the absence of private tutoring, to be molded for their inevitable roles as wives.

"You don't know how disappointed I am in you," Mother said.

"I'm not exactly overjoyed with myself either."

"Maybe you should become a priest," Father proposed in his detached, lighthearted way. He lowered his paper to glance at me. "You've got no career, no commitments, and you're probably too old to make a child anyway. As a priest, you could enjoy your food and wine, and I'm sure you could have women on the side."

I laughed uneasily, trying not to yield to the desperation I felt. With Father once again absorbed in his reading and Mother maintaining a glum silence, I saw a chance to make my break. "Why don't I start this new career by saying a prayer for us all," I said as cheerfully as I could while heading for the door. "Whatever the case, I'm sure it can't hurt."

As best I could reconstruct from having gone as a child, I judged the mass to be about halfway through when I arrived. I remained standing in the back, partly obscured by one of the pillars in a spot where it was dark. I could see the goings on yet remain relatively unseen and hide that consummate sadness I felt since waking up.

The church was filled to capacity. The parishioners were from the area where we had our farm; mainly working families employed at the toilet seat factory and at the state epileptic hospital. Dressed in their Sunday best, the women at first glance looked the way I remembered them as my customers from the summers I had delivered milk. I thought I recognized Mrs. Womek, who used to take three homogenized and one heavy cream in the shade on the back porch. She had just married then, and now was surrounded by her grown children, in laws, and grandchildren filling an entire pew.

I found myself irrationally beset by the scene. During my sporadic visits home over the past quarter century, I hadn't interacted with these people beyond exchanging polite greetings on the street. Now, as I watched their children fidgeting and being pacified by a gentle pat of a parental hand, I could feel the preciousness of their family ties. I was mournfully overwhelmed to realize they possessed something I could never have. I had to suppress an urge to rush up to them and individually congratulate them on being the most fortunate people in the world. If I'd had the chance, I would have at that moment willingly made a commitment to the homeliest of the women in those pews. They were hardly the types seen at the trendy Le Club or listed in *The New York Social Register*. Yet there wasn't a one of them who didn't look becoming in my eyes.

Blinking back an upwelling of tears, I felt I had forever forfeited my chance of having a family. I knew it made no sense, and I tried to reason with myself, but to no avail. Was this what it meant to be condemned to hell? To see something that had for so long been freely offered suddenly taken away and forever removed from your reach?

Standing in the back of the church, I no longer cared if some of the parishioners happened to see me dab at the rivulets glistening on my cheeks. My sole relief throughout the remainder of the mass came while on my knees on the cold stone floor, shutting out reality with the anguished repetitious mumbling, *God, forgive me; forgive me, oh God. I've sinned, even if I didn't know what I was doing, I've so foolishly sinned!*

By the time I returned from church, Mother had finished preparing the usual roast duck for Sunday lunch. Also as usual, she had prevailed on Father to clear his papers off the Renaissance table for this one meal each week, and then set two place mats where he and I would sit. Mother herself preferred to eat from a tray in the adjoining living room, where she could sit in her favorite stuffed chair and be more alone with her thoughts. While she and Father depended on each other in the special way of people who had been together for almost half-a-century, the butcher's daughter never bridged the gulf between her and the illustrious nobleman she married. Even though Father was selling fitness equipment by making house calls, Mother still felt he belonged to a different, privileged world. Intensely proud and jealous in her youth, she no longer allowed herself to wonder about her husband's chronically roving eye and his absences of several days on business in Boston. And she had yet to reconcile herself with living permanently in the United States. She alone in the family never gave up hope that we would one day return *home*. She alone declined to become a U.S. citizen, at first claiming she would be depriving my underage younger brother Tom of his title, since he would automatically become a U.S. citizen along with her. She stoically ignored our mildly derisive arguments that all titles in Czechoslovakia had been abolished long ago, and we would never be going back anyway. After Tom turned eighteen and became a citizen on his own, Mother continued to balk as if becoming naturalized was tantamount to betraying the country of her birth, for which she continued to pine. What finally prompted her to file for citizenship without delay was her first Social Security check. It was for more than three hundred dollars – an astronomical sum considering that she had been saving nickels and dimes from her household budget to add regularly to her savings in the bank. Such unexpected largesse, Mother felt, required a show of loyalty in return – though she never stopped mulling over this decision, along with most of the other decisions she had made throughout her life.

I had never protested Mother's desire for solitude, yet the notion of us being in any way separated now was causing me distress. The sense of impending loss I had felt earlier, I realized, entailed being deprived of my parents as well. I was desperate for us to be together, and a separation of even a few feet seemed unbearable.

"Why can't we for a change all eat at the dining room table," I said, trying to sound casual, "the way other people do?"

Father laughed. "Since when have you wanted to be like other people?"

Mother seemed more amenable to my request. "Always trying to change things," she fretted, "now that I've got everything on my tray."

"Please?" I said quietly, in an attempt to keep my voice from choking, "I'd really appreciate it."

Mother's worried expression deepened. She stood up, and without uttering a word, brought her tray to the table.

I tried not to betray the disproportionate gratitude I felt. As I watched Mother transfer her plates and utensils onto a placemat she had set at the other end of the table from Father, I could understand what it meant for someone to have a last meal with those he loved, be it a businessman convicted of fraud about to report for a stiff term in jail, or a migrant laborer leaving his family to earn sustenance in places unknown. What a privilege to be sitting in the warmth of this home with the two people most precious to me in the world; what a memory to sustain me in whatever lay ahead.

I tried several times to put my emotions into words. But each time, I choked up before I could make a sound. Whatever my fate, I wanted to let my parents know what had always been implicit but I had never said outright: I loved them and was grateful for everything they had done for me in life.

"I don't understand what's happening to me," I finally blurted out, "or what is going to happen . . ."

"That's nothing to be dramatic about," Father said breezily. "You're now eating your lunch, and I think afterwards you'll go back to reading the Sunday paper."

I wanted to clutch him by the arm and feel his closeness for one last time. But he would have taken it as a symptom of my irrationality and shaken me off. In his life, Father had surmounted dramatic turns of fortune and made much harder choices than I, whether crashing his car into an oncoming truck to avoid sharing a platform in the Sudetenland during the war with a Nazi *Gauleiter*, or defying his rational instincts to marry Mother, whose parochial outlook and lack of languages could hold him back from a political career. He chose to face the uncertainties of bringing his wife and five children to the United States and endured whatever it took to provide for his family; whether failing to keep up in our dairy with the steaming bottle washing machine, wearing the blue pinstriped pants from one of his Savile Row suits, with glass shattering and hot water squirting in his face; or elegantly suited up that evening, trying to convince late into the night some staff sergeant at nearby Westover Air Reserve Base of the benefits of buying a life insurance policy. The situation at one point had become so dire that Father lugged to a Boston pawn shop as security for a fifty-dollar loan a mahogany chest with a massive silver setting for twenty-four, custom made some hundred years earlier by Vienna's leading silversmith. No wonder Father would at times crinkle his cheeks until his eyes became slits. Yet Father persisted, no doubt having been built of sterner stuff than I. Despite his incomparably more opulent childhood, Father had been brought up with cold showers, a habit he continued to this day. And while we shared the same distinctive features, a gently sloping forehead and a nose with a slight bump and a suggestion of a cleft at the tip that gave us both an expression of sensuality and zeal, this commonality made me feel closer yet in a sense also more removed, as if I were a mere knock-off of the genuine article. Had I perhaps been spoiled by my doting grandfather, the burly butcher whom I loved (and my grandmother, too!)? He had brought up Mother to handle the vicissitudes that would inevitably come her way in life. But he treated us children as if he were the custodian of some royal brood destined for the genteel existence he imagined would be our lot as future counts.

Was that what Mother had meant when she tried to take responsibility for my skewed outlook on life?

I watched Father take a sip of his daily bottle of beer with his usual gusto. "I know I've never said this before . . ." I started once more, but failed to continue when I felt both of my parents suddenly glancing up. I could sense that such maudlin talk was the last thing they wanted to hear.

"I think the duck this time was a little dry," Mother interjected.

Father put down his knife and fork next to the bones remaining on his plate. "I can't wait for Mother's cake," he announced, then turned to me. "Are you going to make the coffee?"

I realized the moment had come and gone. Having forfeited the chance to express what I had so desperately wanted to, I was at least determined to make the best cup of coffee I could, with exactly the amount of sugar and cream Father liked. As for Mother, maybe I could help her later with the dishes without being obvious about it.

Standing alone in the kitchen by the stove, I felt momentarily free to vent my grief.

8/

It took all the self-control I had to make it through the rest of the day without openly breaking down. What a relief to be once more ensconced in my room for the night, where I didn't have to rein in my distress.

I continued to console myself by attributing my condition to some malfunction of the brain, whether a bona fide mental disorder, or the normally taciturn right side of the brain speaking its mind, as I knew could happen under extreme stress. Whatever the case, I had lost touch with reality as I had always perceived it in the past. The harsh new horizon looming before me was separating me from the world I knew and loved. With each passing moment, I felt myself drifting further and further away from familiar ground.

As I sat there in bed, leaning against the fluffed-up pillows, I was impervious to the softness of the old cashmere turtleneck against my chest and the feel of the fresh cotton sheets directly against my lower half. My body seemed to belong to somebody else, and the mere thought of any sensual stimulus was taboo to me now. It was so uncontestably clear why priests might want to remain celibate! Far from seeing it as an extreme and unnecessary privation, I recognized it as an essential minimum for the priestly state. Only someone without a true calling might deign to question that. After all, how could anyone pursuing personal pleasures or caring for a family devote himself selflessly to serving God and his human flock? How essential it was to keep one's mind on God rather than focusing on some personal goal. There simply was no way to intertwine the two. From what I could remember about Saint Augustine, this church father hadn't gone far enough in merely requiring abstention from sex. Although it made me shudder in revulsion and fear, I could appreciate the more extreme of the saints; those who had retired to the desert to sit for decades on a little perch, famished and exposed to the elements, their bodies slowly rotting away. Why, even Saint Francis, with his terrible privations and bleeding stigmata was pursuing that inexorable path only in a moderate way.

As I continued to be subsumed by this alien frame of mind, I could understand why the Church had occasionally flirted with strictures against graven images, and why Moslems had in fact outlawed such materialistic fluff from their mosques and worshipping rituals. I could see how the most innocent pictorial renderings could escalate in dangerous ways. I only needed to glance at myself in those photos on the wall. They were all immoral and in one way or another led to sin. Especially that large color blowup on Bermuda's Elbow Beach, glorifying the human flesh which had so enslaved me and made me a puppet of my desires. To think of the effort I had expended to maintain and beautify this physical self, while it was gradually destroying the essence of who I was! Rather than living for me, my body had tricked me to live for it. How could I have considered taking some of these pictures to Florida to decorate the walls of my new apartment in Coconut Grove? That would be blasphemy of the crassest sort, perpetuating my sinful ways from which I was being increasingly removed. If I ever did manage to resume a normal life and return to Florida, I would have to leave behind even the etchings of my ancestors with their arrogant airs, pretentious uniforms, and frilly, degenerate clothes. What a spectacle of pathetic pride! I would, of course, have to leave behind most of my magazines and books, with their immoral, seductive ideas; not just the few pornographic ones expressly designed to titillate, but also the informative ones, such as *Newsweek* and *Time*, so replete with suggestive attitudes, stories, and ads. First thing the next day I would have to get rid of them all, along with all the boxes of letters, pictures, and trinkets I had accumulated over the years. They were a reflection of a life that was no longer mine and were better discarded as so much waste.

Yes, I could see what terminal horrors the world was heading for with such blatant appeals to the eyes in films and on TV and everywhere you looked, promoting sex and virtually every physical desire, appetite, or want. The forthcoming conflagration loomed no less imminent than the gruesome prophecies of biblical fundamentalists. No wonder the ayatollahs in Iran were running wild, veiling their women in black, throwing suggestive music off the air, and otherwise purging their society of these evils of sensuality that inevitably led to disastrous ends. They were only doing what was right and shouldn't be vilified. I could understand why the horrors of the medieval inquisition chamber once had a constructive role, and indeed, had been designed to save the sinner from paying a more terrible price. Who knew what tortures I might have to undergo to pay for my sins? A short stretch on an inquisitor's rack between my sophomore and junior years at Yale might have spared me a lot. It all made sense, now that I was possessed by this primitive, righteous spirit that demanded a return to the most basic of laws; laws that were unmerciful yet so necessary and just, at least as they were being applied to me. Only my lifelong attitude of live-and-let-live and abhorrence of overt violence kept me from feeling obliged to sally forth and force on others the rigid standards that held me in their throes. They were for me alone to submit to, I repeated to myself.

Sitting there in bed, entranced by these thoughts, I was seized with a missionary zeal. If only there was a way to shout a warning to keep others from following my path! Whatever was happening to me could happen to millions of similarly unwitting souls. My transgressions had derived from merely following the popular mantra of our times, *You only go around once; so get all the pleasures you can.* If only somebody had warned me in a persuasive way, as my boarding school headmaster, the Duke, had tried to do when he finally saw through me just before I graduated from his school. He was the one person who knew how to attack human flaws. The various churches and self-styled moralists, alas, always sounded self-righteous, pompous, and out of date, and their homilies were more likely to bore than inspire or instill fear.

Before turning out the bedside light, I glanced at the photo of Katherine on my dresser. There was the same diabolic flicker in her eyes that I had noticed several nights before. Wasn't it possible Katherine had been partly possessed, like the witches of old? After all, isn't that what witches were — super-sensuous women whose uncontrolled moans in the throes of passion had been overheard by vigilant neighbors?

I wasn't astonished at this bizarre thought that was helping me realize how much Katherine and I had been alike. Her desire for the narcosis of pleasure must have been as strong as mine; indeed, perhaps stronger, making it doubly inevitable for our relationship to end up with nowhere to go.

Taking care to avoid eye contact with her demonic look, I forsook the warmth of my bed to turn Katherine's photo face down on the dresser top. I opened the frost-covered window and switched off the table light. As I stood in the dark by my bed, arms upraised and begging God to help me in some way, I could feel the cold seeping around my body. I contemplated for a moment what it would be like if I remained praying all night, but then was back under the covers again. As soon as I began to feel their protective warmth, I jumped out of bed once more, and with arms upraised, continued to implore God for a few moments more in the penetrating cold.

Twice more I succumbed to this compulsive pattern before wrapping myself in the blankets and waiting for sleep to release me for the night.

9/

The next morning, I knew. It was well before daybreak when I suddenly sat up with a start. It was as if someone had passed through the room. The window was still open but the clarity of the message made me impervious to the cold.

How presumptuous to have thought God wanted me to become a priest or a monk! I had considered it a punishment to be a servant of God. Now, I could see what an honor it would have been; an honor for which I couldn't begin to qualify, certainly not before paying the price.

Now, I knew what I had to do. There was no mistaking the message. I understood why I had felt the way I did the day before; why I sensed I would never see my parents again; why during church I thought my chances for a married life had been forfeited for good. How right I had been, because all that was to be a part of the price.

Yes, it was so clear now! I was to leave home right away; not tomorrow, not this afternoon, but early this morning to get a good start. I had a long day ahead in the wintry cold. I was to pack a little suitcase, preferably an older one, with only the necessities that would keep me clothed. I was to take no more than two hundred dollars and leave everything else behind; leave behind my little hatchback car; the custom-made suits, whether from Sills of New York or London's Savile Row; leave behind whatever money I had, the twenty-thousand-dollars-or-so that had heretofore served as an insurance policy against having to indenture myself to some less-than-pleasant job. That option, obviously, I would no longer need.

My marching orders were to hitchhike the 150-odd-miles to New York, wherever my ride would let me off. From there, I was to take a subway to the Bowery or a similar neighborhood frequented by old hoboes and drunks. I was to seek out the nearest shelter or charity home and volunteer my services. I was to work there with the derelicts, mopping up their puke, dressing their ulcerated skin, or just speaking to them a few kind words. And I was to get a job as a short-order cook in some cheap, all-night eatery; maybe one of the White Towers, a chain I knew for the garish lights and starkly white decor of their franchises. Of the money I earned, I was to keep just enough to subsist. If it turned out I couldn't stay at the shelter and had to get a place of my own, it was to be one of those cold-water walk-up rooms I had occasionally seen in depressing movies with a filthy metal sink, a single element hot plate, a narrow army cot, and dangling from the ceiling, a bare electric bulb. The rest of the money from the White Tower job I was to spend on the derelicts.

I sat rigidly in bed, the icy blasts gusting in through the open window. What a terribly ingenious punishment! Even my culinary talents would be put to use! Not that there was anything in these orders I could modify or change. They had been delivered with the same uncompromising resolve as when I had first been told of my sins, and then commanded not to eat that meal. There was no bargaining possible, no questioning allowed. This was something that had to be done, an obligation to be discharged, the price to be paid. The purpose was not so much for me to help others at this stage. That was incidental to the far more personal mission I had to undertake: to learn to submit, to atone, to subjugate myself, to give up the self. I would be starting at the lowest rung among those aspiring to serve God. Only after years of this annealing process could I be ready for the honor of becoming a priest or a monk, or doing similar exclusive service to God. But I didn't need to worry about that. God would let me know in no uncertain way. He had the means, just as he was so clearly directing me what I had to do now.

Oh, no! I wailed half aloud and slid deep under the covers. What had I gotten myself into? Was this God's answer to the uncertainty I had begged him to resolve? I pressed my eyes shut and tried to make my brain go blank. But there was that implacable command again: BETTER GET GOING . . . REMEMBER, YOU NEED TO GET AN EARLY START.

Outside, the darkness had softened and the first bluish wisps of dawn began to delineate sky from land. How I wished that light would never come and I could slip into the restfulness of a dark oblivion that would protect me until all of this went away. More so than on any day of my life, I dreaded getting up to face the world; the world that had always looked so inviting, full of welcome surprises and treats. How bleak and cold it now appeared through the still-open window, beneath the frosted panes of glass. The heavy, dark clouds seemed overstuffed with snow. What would I wear? What would I pack in the little suitcase that would be most useful for what I had to do? Thank God I had a lot of skiing things for blustery weather on the slopes. I could perhaps start out wearing my thermal underwear and woolen socks. The old sheepskin coat covering the lower part of my bed would come in handy, too. Lucky I hadn't thrown it away. It had rubbed through in several spots and I wore it only at home. Yet it had once kept me warm in the best of style. I remembered wrapping it around my head in the plush first-class compartment of the overnight Paris-Munich express to separate myself from other well-turned-out passengers gathered there for the night. Now, I might have to use it at night to separate myself in the derelict ward from what was to be my new world of drunks and other unfortunates of life. Maybe I would get a corner bed, where I might at least have the privacy of two walls.

I tried to bury my head beneath the two pillows on my bed. But that uncompromising command once more sprung me into a sitting position. HURRY UP, HURRY UP . . . YOU HAVE NO TIME TO WASTE!

I could smell the coffee aroma drifting in through the crack under the closed door. Mother was having her breakfast. Father would be up shortly to do his hour of exercises, and then have his breakfast about the same time as I normally would. God, what to tell my parents? Thanks for everything, I'm leaving, I won't ever see you again?

I felt myself whirl into a posture that was becoming familiar by now: on my knees, hands clasped over my chest, and head bowed in silent prayer. *God, if I have to do what I have to do . . . give me the strength to do it . . . give me the grace and the courage to go through with this test . . . just like you gave your son, Jesus Christ. Please, God, give me strength . . . strength which I never had . . . strength to follow the hard road. You know what a sucker I've been for the soft road. But I see it's your road I have to travel now. God, give me that special spirit . . . your spirit . . . to make it through. Protect me and don't leave me . . . hold my hand and help carry me through.*

I had never prayed with such intensity before. I must have been on my knees only a few minutes, but by the time I finished I was strangely calm. I didn't feel happy, yet neither did I feel sad in the same way as before. I felt accepting of my fate, un-afraid and strong, almost serene. Somehow, I knew everything would be all right; that I would get a ride to New York; that I would find a homeless shelter with a spare bed. And right around the corner would be that White Tower with a HELP WANTED sign. I could start right away. Within twelve hours, I would be settled into a new life, irreversibly separated from my former world as if guillotined yet able to survive. I had a powerfully lib-erating feeling that my own well-being didn't matter, even my life didn't matter. I had only one purpose. To do what I had to do. To do the right thing, the will of God . . . and thereby earn salvation.

Despite this protective trance suffusing me with strength and resolve, I remained aware of what I was going through. "Hmm,"

I said to myself, from within that comforting cocoon, "so this is what's meant by the Holy Spirit of the Lord descending on you from above. It really does work! Oh God, thank you, thank you, oh God."

As I faced Mother across the table in the kitchen nook, I already had on my sheepskin coat. For a moment we sat in silence. She was finishing her second cup of coffee and lit her morning cigarette. Her solitary breakfast was perhaps the most consistent pleasure in her life over the past thirty years. Now, each of us was sizing up the situation.

It was Mother who spoke first, employing one of her standard lines as if nothing unusual was happening. "How can you walk around the house in such a heavy coat? I don't want to have to play nurse if you get sick."

"That's all right, Mother. I'll be leaving soon."

"So early?" she asked in a normal tone. "Where're you going this time?"

"Away," I said, with a finality that surprised me.

Mother took a puff on her cigarette. Exhaling slowly, she was momentarily obscured by billows of smoke.

"I'm going to New York," I continued. "To the Bowery. I've got to go there to work with hoboes and drunks."

Mother blew away the smoke and looked at me as if I had turned quietly insane.

"I know it sounds crazy," I said, feeling that strange calm within. "But look at me. Don't I look all right?"

She nodded. "But you sound crazy."

As best I could, I explained my plan for hitchhiking to New York and starting a new life.

"But you can't do that," she said, as if grasping at the most visible straw. "Hitchhiking is against the law in Massachusetts. You know that!"

I couldn't help an ironic smile. "I'll be doing God's will. He'll be watching out for me."

"God's will?" Mother asked bitterly.

"He told me this morning . . . around five. I thought I'd have more time to prepare myself. But I guess he's getting impatient. The message I got this morning was that there was to be no more fooling around."

Mother put down her cigarette. She looked as if she was about to go into shock. "What is happening to you!"

"I'm trying to work out my salvation," I said, surprised at my own answer.

Mother looked incredulous. "Your salvation?"

"I've broken many commandments," I continued. "You've often witnessed that yourself."

"So what? Even priests break them today. It's nothing unusual."

"I now understand what you meant whenever you said I had a skewed outlook on life. It's frightening how clearly I know what God wants me to do. At last I know. For the first time in my life, I know. And right now, he wants me to go to the Bowery to do that work. I have no choice."

"If you really feel you've got to do that," Mother said, making an effort to sound matter-of-fact, "you can do it right here at the state hospital. I'm sure working with the epileptics there is no picnic. But at least you won't have to go anywhere."

I shook my head. "I couldn't begin to do here what I have to do. It's far too comfortable . . . my nice bed, the fireplace, my wonderful meals, you and Dad. Don't you think I love it here?

But as I said, I have no choice. Part of my mission is precisely to leave everything behind, never to return or in any way look back, and start a new life where my own comforts or preferences no longer matter."

Mother abruptly ground out her cigarette. "Well, don't come running to me when you get sick," she said, with feigned impatience. She paused, then in a calmer tone gave me the practical reasons why I couldn't leave: I had signed the apartment lease in Coconut Grove, and I had to write those daycare center scripts. "And don't forget, you have a ten o'clock appointment to have your car oil changed."

I felt a sad smile on my lips. When I didn't immediately respond, Mother continued, "Surely you can't be as irresponsible as all that. Surely you can't let all those people down."

"What if I suddenly died?" I asked gently.

"What if trees could fly?" Mother countered.

"I'm sure dying is more common than what's happening to me now."

"That doesn't mean you should tempt fate. Among those derelicts, you could get stabbed, who knows, perhaps even . . ."

"Don't you see, that's irrelevant?" I interrupted. "I'm not going there for my health. I'm going there to start the life of the spirit. As of now, forget my body."

"But that's wrong, wrong, wrong!" Mother wailed. "You're still young, you're good looking, you've got everything to live for."

I nodded. "Above all, my salvation."

"What about your parents? Don't you have a responsibility to us?"

"That's what pains me the most," I said, feeling an upwelling of emotion, yet remaining calm on the outside. "Somehow, I knew yesterday I'd be saying a final good bye. That's why I wanted us to eat together. I also wanted to tell you . . ."

I paused, struggling to say what I had left unsaid the day before. Despite my apparent fortitude, I could feel a tear worm its way down my cheek. "I just wanted you to know how much I love you and Dad . . . even if I didn't always show it."

The tears were now running down Mother's cheeks. During our family's early years of penury, she had always hidden her tears, as if it were an emotion she couldn't afford. The only time I had seen her openly give vent to a veritable flood was in the early years of our economic travails, when she sought to obtain better terms for Father before signing off on the sale of a saw mill that had failed to pan out.

I reached over and did something I had never done before. I took her aging, gnarled hand in mine and held it gently. "I realize you always knew what I was feeling," I said, "but this is so different. It's as if . . . as if it wasn't me speaking. Don't you see, we all live only by the grace of God. What if God took me from you in an automobile accident, and I was in the state I'm in now? Can you imagine what eternal damnation is all about? I know I'll never see you again, but you're not losing me. I'll be working for my salvation, for my next life."

For a moment, Mother didn't respond. She drew a paper napkin from a dispenser on the table and dried each of her cheeks in a single motion.

"I don't suppose you've told Father?" she asked.

"I won't leave before he gets up."

This seemed to make my departure more real, and after a moment of silence, fresh tears started to roll down Mother's cheeks.

"Don't you see," I resumed, "I'm gradually being called to enter the City of God. It's a great honor. But the road from the City of Man, with its temporary pleasures and concerns, isn't easy. We get so easily deceived . . ."

I paused, again surprised at what I was saying. Were these words coming from some ethereal source outside my brain, or was my memory being nudged at this critical juncture in life to recall some of what I had absorbed about Saint Augustine in Professor Baumer's class more than a quarter century ago?

Mother's voice brought me out of my ruminations. "At least have some breakfast," she said, in an effort to sound normal, and crumpled up the paper napkin in her hand.

Gently, I released Mother's hand and stood up. "I think I need to go to the bathroom," I said, and quickly headed upstairs. I was still feeling that special spirit and strength which was continuing to sustain me. But a part of me, the visceral part, was taking its toll.

The spiritual trance seemed to remain unimpaired as I flushed the toilet, pulled up my long johns and pants, and started to wash my hands. I held them under the pleasantly warm water, thinking of the piercing weather outside in which I would have to hitch a ride.

Just then I caught a glimpse of myself in the mirror above the sink. I could barely recognize the waxen image. In the days of feeling great, looking in the mirror reinforced that positive feeling. At the moment, I figured it was just as well I couldn't establish rapport with that sallow reflection; it kept me from recognizing the desperate straits I was in.

I was about to turn off the hot water when I suddenly detected a familiar glimmer in the vacant eyes staring back at me. That snapped the trancelike state, and I was looking at myself again. At the same time, a new message was distinctly impressing itself on my consciousness: YOU DON'T HAVE TO GO. NOW

THAT YOU HAVE PROVED YOUR INTENTION, YOU NO LONGER HAVE TO DO IT.

I don't have to go! I don't have to go! I repeated to myself. The words continued to echo within my mind like a crescendo of peeling church bells spreading the good news. I don't have to go! I don't have to go! I don't have to go!

I remembered what had happened several days earlier, when I started to put away my meal. I no longer had to, once I had shown my intention to comply. Was it the same thing now? I had honestly forgotten about that unwitting ploy, which had served either to fool the psyche or get a dispensation from the powers beyond.

I kept the hot water running on my hands for an instant more, luxuriating in its warmth. For the first time, I was relating to the image in the mirror and how awful I looked. My face was sallow and I had deep hollows around the eyes, almost as if I had stepped out of a grave. Thank God the dispensation had come! I managed a little smirk at my image before bolting out of the bathroom and rushing downstairs with the good news.

Father was already doing his leg raises in his underwear on the living room floor. Nothing could normally interrupt his routine, but seeing me, he paused to give me a reproachful look. "What's this nonsense of yours that Mother's been telling me about?"

"I don't have to go," I said with excitement. "It's all right. I don't have to go."

"You shouldn't scare your poor mother that way," Father chided me, and then resumed his exercising as if nothing of consequence had happened.

In the kitchen, Mother was taking the unprecedented step of lighting her second cigarette. "Come on, have some breakfast," she said numbly. "I'm going upstairs. I've had it for the day."

10/

My peace of mind didn't last long. Shortly after breakfast, I started to have that unpleasant feeling again, as if somebody was forcibly kneading my guts, and an increasingly persistent message was beginning to get through. BETTER GET GOING! BETTER GET GOING WHILE THERE IS TIME . . . OR FACE THE CONSEQUENCES FOR AS LONG AS ETERNITY LASTS.

Not again! My response this time was to protest, having just recalled a biblical precedent for what I was going through: how God had stayed Abraham's hand from sacrificing his only son after Abraham proved his willingness to do just that. God certainly didn't tell Abraham a few hours later that he had changed his mind. So why pick on me? Hadn't I made my willingness to obey amply clear?

That's what was beginning to worry me. Had I truly intended to go when I received that reprieve? The most objective proof was that I had put on the long johns in anticipation of my hitch-hiking ordeal. I normally wore them only under skiing pants for riding chair lifts on freezing days. But I recalled putting them on for other occasions, too. Besides, I was an excellent dissimulator. I could have put them on just to pretend I intended to go.

I started to walk around the living room, sporadically rubbing my temples and crinkling my eyes. Would my salvation depend on exactly why I had decided to wear my thermal long johns that day? What was my life coming to?

BETTER GET GOING, IT'S GETTING LATE! YOU MUST LEAVE NOW TO GET TO NEW YORK BEFORE DARK . . .

The message wasn't hitting me with the swift, sharp blows as it had at dawn. It seemed to have been engraved on a heavy tablet of stone and dropped into my abdominal cavity, making me feel uncomfortably cramped and providing a constant reminder of its intrusive presence there.

I made an exaggerated grimace, and several times banged the palms of my hands against the sides of my head, as if trying to jar my memory.

"Aren't you ashamed of yourself?" Mother said, after watching me for a while. She sensed that the danger of my leaving had passed, and firmness was the best approach. "Get ahold of yourself! I think what you're doing to yourself is a sin."

"Oh, you don't understand," I said, gritting my teeth. "Would you dare turn God down?"

"Why don't you stop this nonsense and go get your car oil changed," Mother suggested sternly.

I couldn't keep the pain from showing on my face. Mother's reference served as a poignant reminder that I should have been on my way.

"It's all in your head," Father suggested, with an easy wave of the hand. He had promised Mother to skip his usual drive to his Exercycle office in Boston and stay home to keep an eye on me. He was poking through some of the papers he had already dumped back on the Renaissance table since Sunday's lunch. "Maybe what you've got is a form of *Platz angst*," Father said, without interrupting his paperwork chores. "Just as I always predicted, but I never thought you'd get it this bad. You'll end up like my old uncle Serge, yet."

"I know, I know," I said impatiently. This wasn't the first time I had been given the example of Uncle Serge, an old bachelor who had been the laughingstock of the family when Father was growing up. Platz angst meant literally fear of place or agoraphobia, but the designation was used more as a fashionable catchall to explain the eccentricities of the noble rich. Poor people obviously couldn't indulge such symptoms as being terrified of throngs of other common folk. Platz angst sufferers had their carriages draped when traversing public squares, and if caught unawares, they might wrap themselves in horse blankets or pull up their coats or dresses as a shield. "I'd rather have Platzangst any day than what I've got."

"Tell me again," Father said with total lack of seriousness, "what exactly is it that you've got? I'm afraid I still don't understand."

"Isn't it obvious?" I groaned. "I'm fighting the will of God. I've failed to carry out His commands."

"Maybe I'm dumb," Father said, "but what makes you so sure it's God telling you these things?"

"I know, I just know," I said, continuing my anxious pacing of the living room. Of course it was God! Who else but? Those messages sounded exactly like the Old Testament God I still remembered from our daily chapel readings in boarding school; the just but angry Yahweh, inexorably stern with those who dared disobey his word.

Yet that's what was puzzling me now. How come the Jesus I had briefly experienced at Manya's prayer meeting had been so gentle and comforting? Wasn't Jesus the same as God, an integral part of an indivisible Trinity? How could God then be so demanding and stern? You'd think that if the Trinity were to have credibility, the various entities would have gotten their act together by now. Maybe Father did have a point. Maybe my mind was playing dangerous tricks. From what I had read, I knew how implacable a guilty conscience could be; how it could demand even self-mutilation and suicide, or turn its vengeance on the world. Almost every week, there were stories in newspapers and on TV of individuals claiming that God had told them to do this and that, from grisly murders to hijacking of planes and countless other nonsensical acts. I had dismissed such people as deranged, acting under irrational impulses from the brain. Yet they must have been every bit as convinced of their divine inspiration as I — indeed, far more so to have carried out their acts.

The possibility that I was merely deranged seemed to have a calming effect. I stopped pacing and sat down on the living room couch. Yes, I needed to have additional proof; proof that it really was God ordering me around. Even in the Bible, God had occasionally given proof. Like when Saul of Tarsus had been blinded on his way to persecute Christians in Damascus, and then regained his sight as he started speaking out for Christ as St. Paul. Not that I needed anything so dramatic, or that I saw myself as a future saint. I was a miserable reprobate who had barely seen the light and wanted to be left alone.

I realized proof in this area wasn't easy to come by in our age of skepticism and doubt. If God in his familiar guise as the Creator on the Sistine Chapel ceiling appeared at a psychiatric convention, delivered the keynote address, and walked out through a closed door, those scientific-minded sophisticates could quickly figure out how to dismiss what they had witnessed as a subjective mass delusion. I needed something more substantial than my perception of those celestial messages; something that would stand up to hard, objective scrutiny.

But what, God, what?

83

Why not numbers? I suddenly thought. Weren't numbers our most reliable tool for ascertaining reality throughout the universe? Surely, if God could communicate to me his detailed message about hitchhiking to New York, taking a subway to the Bowery, and all the rest, he could communicate a few authenticating numbers as well.

I stood up and once more started to pace the living room floor.

Okay, so it's numbers, I said to myself, but which ones? Where do I begin?

Just then, I realized I was standing by the window sill, where more of Father's papers were messily stacked. (Brought up with servants and butlers who had picked up in his trail, Father was oblivious to this mess, much to Mother's lifelong chagrin.) I reached into the nearest pile and started to grope around. My intent was to pull out at random some document with a number on it and try to match it with a number in my head.

I was still trying to formulate that number when I heard Father say, "I'll thank you to stay out of my papers and not mess up everything."

Respectful of Father's ability to readily fish out from his mess whatever he was looking for, I resumed my nervous pacing, trying to figure out what to do. But then Mother had a suggestion. "Why don't you do something useful," I heard her through my fog, "and get that oil changed? You're already late."

11/

It was almost noon by the time I returned home, the car oil good for another 5,000 miles. While in town, I also took care of several errands at the library, hoping to ease the internal tension I felt.

But that stern, nonnegotiable command continued to press heavily within. GET GOING! SUBMIT TO MY WILL . . . OR FOREVER FACE MY WRATH.

Lunch wasn't for another hour yet. Maybe a walk in the woods would help. I was leery about what had befallen me the last time I ventured there, but I figured the chances of anything of that sort happening again were about as unlikely as two consecutive aviation disasters on the same route. "Come on, Blackie," I said, opening the cellar door, "Let's go!"

Outside it was cold, with an unpleasant dampness in the air. A leaden sky looked as if it might drop of its own insupportable weight and smother everything below.

Blackie was oblivious of my depressed mood. Joyful to be outside with human company, he raced ahead on the narrow forest path as if he were a scout. After his exuberant foray, he settled down no more than a dozen yards ahead to lead the way. He was getting on in years and showed his affection in an occasional backward glance rather than jumping all over my sheepskin coat.

Absorbed in my distressing thoughts, I was surrounded by the forest's tall evergreens, a sliver of overcast sky making the enclosure complete. I shook my head sharply from side to side, checking on the strange pangs I had been sporadically feeling for several days. It wasn't a headache, but a pain deep within my brain, somewhere in the region of the pituitary. Maybe that's what I had, a pituitary gland tumor. It wasn't that uncommon a condition, I had recently read, and was operable now – a procedure in which the surgeon went in through the nose, boring his way to the base of the skull. Ugh, what people wouldn't do to stay alive, though I didn't really think I had anything surgery could fix. Maybe the pituitary was the means for receiving those messages from beyond, just as it was the center where tranquilizers and sleeping pills often did their work. I had, in fact, considered several times easing the tension this way. But the same warning had always come through: KEEP YOURSELF OPEN TO MY WORD . . . REMEMBER THERE ARE NO TRANQUILLIZERS IN HELL!

"Come on, Blackie, over here," I called, when I saw the old mutt start on another path in the fork ahead instead of the one I wanted to take. But Blackie ignored me, as he often did. I merely shrugged and turned to follow him. Maybe this would prove to be another sign from beyond, I said to myself, with a mixture of despair and jest.

About a hundred yards further on, I came across a rock in my path that I had never noticed before. Judging by the way it was embedded in the ground, it must have been there since the turn of the century, when the area had served as a granite quarry. It wasn't really an obstacle but jutted out enough to make me pause. I was puzzled how this rock could have escaped my attention over the years on my occasional treks.

I looked around. For the first time in the years I had been walking here, I discerned an unused path leading off to the left. Trees and overgrown bushes were partly blocking it, but I could easily get through to the clearing I spotted ahead. Blackie had disappeared on another foray of his own, and I was left to press on alone.

I was in the clearing now. It was peacefully quiet here, except for a gentle hum in the crowns of the trees. Looking up, I saw the sky begin to take on an eerie glow, as if the sun was trying to break through. *Oh God,* I said to myself, *give me a convincing sign in our world of disbelief and competing truths . . . let me know with certitude the meaning of what's been going on.*

The conditions seemed ideal for some kind of a revelation or a miracle to occur. The setting reminded me of a film I had once seen about the peasant children in Portugal who had a vision of the Virgin Mary hovering on the outskirts of their hometown of Fatima. How lucky they had been! They hadn't been to college and had no liberal education to hinder them in matters of this sort. It was easy for them to believe what they had seen. Wasn't that what their eyes were for? How could someone as smart as I end up so helplessly cornered, no longer certain what was and wasn't real?

I was suddenly suffused with a sense of devotion. I felt as if I were standing in a cathedral, with the tall trees becoming the graceful ribs of a soaring medieval nave and the small patch of brightening sky fragmented by the many branches forming a stained-glass window to God. I felt myself sink to the ground and kneel on the hard layer of frozen snow, then raise my arms in a prayerful way. *Now, God, now! Please, the sign, now!*

I was absorbed by the dramatic potential of the moment. All I needed was the sign. Or rather, not to get the sign. If I wasn't going to get the sign under these ideal conditions, I would probably never get it at all. I squinted my eyes to refract the light shimmering in the branches above. Maybe I could help those fragmented rays fall into a revealing pattern or shape; a cross, a face of Christ, or some kind of a symbol of divinity or God. Surely, in the absence of even such a contrived sign, I would be free to resume a normal life.

I was beginning to feel the cold wetness of the snow on my knees, soaking through my pants and long underwear. The sun was becoming obscured by heavy clouds again, and the surrounding woods had reverted to their normal wintry look. The best time for a miracle had obviously passed, and it had failed to materialize.

I lowered my arms and was about to get to my feet, when seemingly from nowhere, Blackie appeared. He startled me by leaping up and putting his paws all over my sheepskin coat. As if that wasn't unusual enough for sedate old Blackie, he was acting in a weird non-dog way. He was nipping away at me and pawing me as if he didn't want me to move from this spot. When I finally struggled to my feet after repeatedly pushing him off, he again started to hurl himself at me to block my way. He took a firm bite of the hem of my sheepskin coat and tried to drag me back. He then bit into my gloves and almost pulled them off.

"Come on, Blackie, what's the matter?" I tried to reason. "Good dog, Blackie, good dog!" It was as if he didn't know who I was. Though neither angry nor affectionate, the mutt continued to charge with a single-minded purpose that he seemed not to understand but was determined to carry out. Never in the years I had been walking with Blackie had I seen him act this way. It just wasn't Blackie. He persisted for at least two minutes more, until I got out of that clearing where I had knelt. Then, as abruptly as he began, he trotted off nonchalantly, good old Blackie again.

I could feel my heart pounding; not from any exertion but because of what was inescapably clear. I felt as if I had blundered into the world of some spooky TV show. Only it was all so terribly real! I suspected all along what it was about, from the instant Blackie had come charging in. I wanted to get out of that clearing as quickly as I could, fearing what might happen if I stayed. Yet what more could have happened to dramatize the sign? The most frightening moment had come at the end, when in a trice, as if on command, Blackie became his old self again and sauntered off as if he no longer cared. That's when I knew what it meant beyond a shadow of doubt, no matter how much I tried to tell myself otherwise.

As I hurried home on the narrow forest path, illuminated by an eerie verdancy refracted from the evergreens, I was gripped by a primitive terror humans experience when face to face with the unknown. Yet I was also feeling a strange elation for having been singled out by the powers beyond. How many saints, from my limited knowledge of their lives, ever had to grapple with an experience of this sort? It certainly surpassed the miracle of Saint Augustine, who, asking for a divine sign in his own spiritual quandary, heard a child's voice sing, "Take up and read" – bringing him to a crucial section of the Holy Writ.

Rushing along the eerie path and thinking of Saint Augustine's revelation, I was beset by a wild idea that nevertheless seemed more and more logical with each step. Was I perhaps seeing those trees and shrubs casting their ghostly shadows, as if illuminated by a light source in eclipse, through the eyes of Saint Augustine? Was I, in fact, Saint Augustine, reincarnated in a modern guise and chosen to follow the very path he had to endure as he wrestled with himself and begged, *God make me chaste, but not yet!* That's exactly how I would have described my condition now. Or was I the one who had been Saint Augustine some fifteen hundred years ago, and Saint Augustine now was me?

As I continued along the forest path in the spectral light, engulfed in my mystical turmoil, I had an altogether different thought. Maybe I was just another megalomaniac taking his act to new heights on a different stage. The world was full of madmen thinking they were saints or Jesus Christ, singled out by God to fulfill some messianic mission on earth. Maybe Blackie's behavior had been nothing unusual, merely a dog bewildered at seeing me act so strange. Maybe I had been sending out in that prayerful position some special Alpha waves that altered dumb Blackie's behavior in such a dramatic way.

On three separate occasions while rushing home, I did a little test. I went down on my knees, and after a few moments of praying fervently I waited to see how Blackie would react. In each case Blackie stopped, and with evident patience but no special interest, watched me from where he stood. When I finally called to him from my kneeling position, he merely trotted up. It took a torrent of encouraging words before he gave me a couple of affectionate sniffs. Then he sat down on his haunches a few feet away, again waiting patiently until I was through. In near desperation, I tried to get him worked up so he would jump up and play a little rough, or engage me in a tug of war for my sheepskin coat or gloves. But to no avail. Blackie continued in his same, apathetic way, without the slightest reminder of the way he had acted in the clearing only moments ago.

If only poor, dumb Blackie with the dry blobs hanging from the long hairs around his tail could have realized how much had been at stake!

12/

"I'm afraid I might have to leave after all," I informed my parents in a trembling voice when I returned.

I tried to explain what had just happened in the woods, but Father cut me short. "How can you talk so stupidly," he snapped, in an uncharacteristic departure from his lighthearted attitude to my ordeal. "Now you really are getting to be worse than old Uncle Serge. Poor Blackie's probably the dumbest dog in town, and you want to base your future on what he does?"

I was tempted to argue that Blackie being dumb was probably more of an asset than a liability for missions of this sort, offering a malleable psyche unhindered by a priori views. Yet, on further reflection, I did have to admit that Blackie's behavior couldn't be quantified into hard, objective evidence. Trap-ped as I was between carrying out God's non-negotiable demands and what I profoundly didn't want to do, my only alternative was to resume the search for evidentiary proof; proof that would either make me willingly submit or release me from my involuntary task.

This meant returning to the mathematical criteria I had set forth prior to the Blackie episode. And here, I intuitively hit on a new technique. I now recalled what I had never paid any attention to before: The afternoon newspaper listed every day ten Social Security numbers selected at random to receive a five-dollar prize each. These were nine-digit numbers, so the chances I would get one right were one in a billion.

On a little slip of paper, I composed a nine-digit number that gradually came into my head. If it turned out I hit the number right on, that would authenticate the source of those messages. I made a solemn pledge in such a case to leave home without delay.

Now, all I could do was wait.

By midafternoon, I was beginning to have second thoughts. The paper should have been delivered by then, and I realized I had miscalculated. Since I had written down only one number, and ten numbers would be printed in the paper today, this reduced the odds by a factor of ten – making it a far riskier gamble than I had assumed.

By four o'clock the paper still hadn't arrived, and I was be-coming increasingly nervous. Who knew where the newspaper boy was; perhaps engaged in some romance of the ten-year-old set, smoking a joint behind the drugstore, or hanging around town with other kids until dark, waiting for something exciting to liven things up. If he only knew in what an agonized state of suspense he was keeping me!

Still no paper by five; and when it hadn't come at six, I was thinking of calling off my bets. After all, how could I be expected to start hitchhiking to New York at this hour? Maybe the fact that the paper hadn't come yet was in itself a sign that I was to refrain from any immediate moves.

Ten minutes later, I heard the click of the mailbox. The boy had stuffed the paper in, then was off on his bicycle before I could ask where the hell he'd been. In a way, I welcomed the delay; for no matter what the numbers, I couldn't possibly leave before the following day. I figured this wasn't a dishonorable modification of my pledge.

I laid the paper on the table in the kitchen nook, my anxiety holding me in a tremulous grip. It was like coming to the bulletin board in my student days and seeing the grades posted for a final exam on which I wasn't sure I had done well. There was nothing I could do – just brace myself.

Quickly, I scanned the numbers, printed in two columns of five, comparing each against the number on the slip in my hand. I got a series of little shocks as I came across several numbers that started with the 014 prefix I had written down, only to dif-fer totally in the digits that remained. I also had a few breathless moments as I saw my number 56 crop up several times in the second group of digits. As for the final four-digit group, here is where my heart palpably paused. Not only did I instantly spot my number among the listed ten, but earlier, in writing down those last four digits my hand had slipped twice and I ended up putting down a different number from the one I had originally had in mind. I remembered telling myself then, with a mixture of apprehension and jest, that God had been guiding my hand. And there, imprinted within that little box in the paper before me, were precisely those final four digits I had written down as a result of those slips.

I sat at the kitchen table in a daze. No, I hadn't hit the number right on. But wasn't it possible that this numerical freak, for which the chances must have been exceedingly remote — maybe thousands or even tens of thousands against one — had a special significance for me? Perhaps it was expecting too much of God to speak with absolute clarity. If God did that, what would be the purpose of faith? Maybe God was willing to go just so far to help a person like me.

I started to walk around the kitchen, rubbing my temples with the fingertips of both hands. I was trying to keep out the reality of what had just occurred.

I didn't hear my parents walk in. I wasn't aware how long they had remained silent before trying to bring me out of my self-induced trance.

"Do you have a headache?" I heard Mother ask cautiously.

I shook my head. "Unfortunately, that's not my problem, not by a long shot."

"Well, then?" Father joined in, an edge creeping into his voice.

"I'm afraid I'm going to have to leave," I said, now fully out of my oblivion and struggling not to succumb to a sudden wave of grief. "I guess I better get my suitcase packed tonight so I can get going first thing in the morning."

"What's all this nonsense again?" Father asked tartly. "I thought we had already settled that."

"I'm afraid the picture has changed. I've been getting more messages.

"Stop this with your crazy messages," Mother said sharply. "I don't want to hear another word about these . . . these fantasies."

I shook my head. "This time I've got proof. Overwhelming evidence that my messages are real. Numbers unfortunately don't lie."

"First you hear voices like Joan of Arc . . ."

"No, no," I corrected Father. "I never said I heard anything."

"Then it was stupid Blackie," Father continued with evident forbearance. "Well, what about these numbers?"

I was ready, in fact, eager to present my proof. I had in my hand the newspaper as well as the slip of paper with the number I had written down. It was evidence that couldn't leave anyone unconvinced.

Father didn't let me finish. "Ach, your numbers are no good!" he exclaimed in utter disdain, as soon as he got the gist. "You'd never win a lottery that way. Any idiot knows that unless you get the exact number, it's no good. There's no such thing as being close." Father paused, then resumed cheerfully. "Now, if you'd really become good at guessing numbers . . ."

I didn't hold it against my parents that they refused to understand. In their non-comprehending way, they were merely trying to help. "I'll miss you both," I muttered, in a tone which let me keep my voice under control. "I'll miss you terribly." I blinked several times to clear my eyes, and when I looked up, my parents were no longer there. They had withdrawn quietly to the living room, where I could hear Father tuning in the evening news.

I propped up my chin in the palms of my hands and glanced through the frost-covered windows wrapped around the kitchen nook. The evening sky was heavily overcast; no doubt, it would snow all night. By first light, there might be more than a foot. I could see myself setting forth from the house, trudging through the drifts to the Massachusetts Turnpike three miles away, my small battered suitcase in hand. It wouldn't be right to have Mother or Father drop me off. I would have to make the final break at our front door and start walking without turning back.

But the more I thought about these details, the more I realized I never would leave. Not unless I was again imbued with the spirit of calm and otherworldly strength that I had experienced early that morning when I first received those orders. Without it, I was too weak, too addicted to the comforts of my world, and far too unwilling to make a complete and permanent break. The chances of my submitting would further diminish with each passing day, moving salvation further and further from my grasp. Was it the decision to truly go that had of itself given me the special grace to be able to see it through? And was it because throughout the day I had never again decided to go that I didn't feel this special grace again?

13/

That evening the relentless assault didn't let up: BETTER GET GO-ING! YOU HAVE AN ENORMOUS PRICE TO PAY . . . START PAYING IT NOW OR FACE ETERNITY IN THE DARK!

My desperate mood drove me to consider an approach I had previously ruled out. Why not phone my sister, I suddenly thought. Manya had served as an instrument to get me into this mess; so, why not see if she could get me out? If she had brought me this far on God's behalf, surely He wouldn't allow her to steer me wrong.

I dialed Manya's number from the kitchen phone, reluctant to compound my parents' worries after all I had already put them through. I listened to the phone ring several times, my apprehension mounting that Manya might not be home. With each additional ring, I became more and more convinced she held the key to my fate.

What a relief to hear her voice!

"We were eating dinner," Manya explained.

"I can call later," I suggested.

"No, no," she countered, with the fervor of a salesperson who has a promising prospect on the line. "I've already finished."

This time, it was my sister who seemed ready to take the lead. "Well, how are you?" she asked. We hadn't talked since my fateful visit, and I could sense her eagerness to hear about the difference Jesus had made in my life.

"I'm afraid not well, Manya. Not well at all."

"Oh?" Her voice betrayed disappointment as well as curiosity.

As briefly as I could, I summarized what had been happening to me. I told her about the messages directing me to work in the Bowery, about Blackie's behavior, and the other proofs authenticating God's word.

Manya didn't say anything until I got to the part about the numbers. "Now stop right there," she said with authority. "You had me puzzled for a while. But now, it's all crystal clear."

I felt myself clutching the receiver. So it was clear to her too! That's what I had been afraid of. The proof was that obvious.

"Don't you see?" she continued. "It's the devil who's after you! God doesn't deal in numbers. That's the work of the devil. Always has been. The Lord doesn't work that way."

"The devil?" I asked hesitantly, caught off guard by hearing this mythical abstraction referred to as reality. Already as a child spending the war in the safety of a small village far from Prague, I had merged the elderly local priest's fearful image of a furry creature wielding a pitchfork with that of the neighboring farmer's teenage son, who used to come to entertain us in the devil's guise on Saint Nicholas's day in expectation of a generous tip. In subsequent years, my image of the devil metamorphosed into an amalgam of portrayals by artists over the centuries as a sort of unrestrained, leering entity endowed with animalistic sensuality. This was in line with the popular expression, *The devil made me do it*, which usually referred to something mischievous rather than evil. I had, in fact, often been called a devil in jest and took it as a compliment. Now, to hear my sister talk of the devil as if he were real simply failed to connect. "I'm afraid I don't understand," I said.

"There's nothing to understand. Numerology is the sign of the devil. Not only do I think so. The Church says so too."

"Why in the world would the devil try to get me to go to skid row and do charity work with a bunch of derelicts?"

"Because he knows you can't do it. He's trying to ruin you. Set you against yourself. Make you crack up."

"Well, he's doing a damn good job of it."

"The devil's probably jealous of your rebirth, of your new potential with Jesus."

"Why wouldn't he command me to do something wild? Hijack a plane, murder somebody . . . wouldn't that meet his goal better?"

97

"The devil is devious. He wants you to think it's God talking. Then he's got you where he wants . . . rejecting God when it really *is* God talking."

Despite my compelling desire to believe Manya, I was exasperated with her reasoning. "That is devious," I said trying not to sound sarcastic.

"Sometimes it's very difficult to tell the difference between the devil's voice and the voice of God. That's why we all need help. Somebody who's got experience, like a priest. It's dangerous for you to try and do it alone."

"It's no use, Manya. You're a dear for trying to help, but I'm afraid I know where those messages came from. And it's not the devil."

There was a pause. "I still think you should see a priest, especially on this numerology thing."

"How then do you explain Blackie going berserk? Just as I was praying for a sign?"

"Well," my sister said, now hesitating, "I don't know. That's why you should see a priest."

"You see, I'm afraid if I don't offer my life to those Bowery hoboes . . . that's it for my salvation."

"That you don't have to do," Manya interrupted decisively. "About that, I am sure."

"You are?" Her certainty on this crucial issue gave me fresh hope.

"Confession. That's all you need. Then a good act of contrition. I'm sure any priest will give you absolution."

"Oh, that!" I said with thinly veiled contempt. I had been hoping for something more original. I still remembered the last time I had gone to confession as a fifteen-year-old, when the priest tried to ascertain whether I had experienced any bodily changes while kissing, which would help him determine if I had committed a sin. I had little confidence that mumbling a few Our Fathers and Hail Marys was an adequate substitute for the debt I had to discharge. How I only wished that it were! I would have gladly done a thousand of each, especially if they weren't too bunched up. "Look Manya," I continued, "how can some old geezer who doesn't know me from Adam forgive me for the last thirty years?"

"Haven't you forgotten something?"

"I have?"

"The suffering of our Lord on the cross! He died for you. He died for your sins. You see, He already paid the price for you. That's why you don't need to go anywhere."

"I don't?"

"Don't you see? Our Lord knew people like you would need his help. None of us can pay for our sins alone. They're too immense. He came to save us from a fate such as yours. He is *your* savior."

"He is?" I countered feebly.

"All you have to do," I heard my sister continue, "is go to confession, and then receive the body of our Lord in holy communion."

"Are you sure? It sounds too easy."

"Not when you think of how much our Lord suffered on the cross. For you. For me. For all of us. But right now, above all, for you. Just imagine, God's only son going through all that for you."

I never had occasion in the past to relate my fate to the agonies endured by Jesus on the cross. In fact, I had often wondered, why all this ado about Christ? Others had died a still harsher death, and I vaguely resented any suggestion that he had died for me.

Now I started to see it in a different light. Yes, yes, it made sense. Christ's blood was the way out of my personal mess! Hearing Manya reiterate her simple explanation over and over again, I felt myself engulfed by mounting waves of gratitude and relief. And maybe there was something to this two-thousand-year unbroken history of the Church, as my departed friend, Fuzzy Sedgwick, had theorized in opting for a deathbed conversion. Who was I to dispute this enduring institution's word?

The intense emotions released a flow of tears. I now understood why only something so excruciating as the suffering endured by Jesus Christ could pay off my staggering debt. But I had a practical thought. "How can I confess thirty years of sins? I could be in that little booth till eternity begins."

"All you need is to make a general confession."

"Isn't it the details they want? Especially in transgressions having to do with sex?" I asked, perking up.

"Well, it might be better if we find someone who understands," my sister conceded, now herself in an upbeat mood, as if she had closed the deal and was merely negotiating the payment terms. "That old priest you've got there might go into shock."

Manya had one more suggestion before hanging up. She wanted me to call Al, who had been the leader at the prayer meeting that started it all. She thought it wouldn't hurt if I checked with him and received a second opinion on my case. "Give me a few minutes. I'll call him and explain who you are. I'm sure he'll tell you exactly the same as I."

That made me nervous. What if this Al character told me I had to go to the Bowery after all? Where would I be then? On the other hand, if he supported my sister's opinion, I would truly be in the clear.

When I returned to the living room, I was in a much better mood. "I just talked to Manya," I announced to my parents. "She said I don't have to go skid row after all."

Mother made a face indicating she wanted no further part in my inanity, but father smiled. "You see! Isn't that what I've been telling you?"

"All I have to do, Manya says, is to go to confession."

Mother looked up. "I don't care what you do. Only please, don't do it here."

"That's all right. Manya will arrange it somewhere near her. Right now she's talking about my case to the man who conducts her prayer meetings. I'm supposed to call him in a few minutes myself."

"What for?" Father wanted to know.

"Just to chat. Look, I'm not out of the woods yet."

"Is he a priest?"

"I think he's a plumber."

"A plumber?" Father repeated. "In that case, you'll probably get good, sound advice."

But Mother shook her head sadly. "Aren't you ashamed? A Yale graduate calling a plumber to find out what to do with his life!"

14/

Well before dawn the following day, I found myself being practically kicked out of bed. It couldn't have been more than five; yet, there I was, being forcibly ejected from beneath the warmth of my blankets into the frigid air coursing through the room. Though barely awake, I came to with lightning speed, as the old message made itself felt with the compelling force of a kick in the rear: WHAT ARE YOU WAITING FOR? GET GOING, GET GOING WHILE YOU STILL HAVE A CHANCE! YOUR TIME IS RUNNING OUT . . .

Oh no, not again! Wasn't this ever going to end? I stood on the ice-cold floor next to my bed, naked except for the old cashmere turtleneck. I looked up in reverent desperation. *Oh, Jesus, help me, Jesus, please help! I can't stand this much longer!*

I lowered my head for a moment of pious contemplation, then took a couple of steps to let the window down and bounded back to bed. At least until the room warms up, I thought to myself.

NO, RIGHT NOW!

I felt that inexorable command shaking me to the core. I burrowed deeper under the covers, as if I could evade that silent voice or pretend it didn't exist, the way I had done with Katherine when she thought I was asleep and articulated her secret hopes over my slumbering form. There was no way I could do it now; no way to ignore or shut out God's insistent message. This led me to agonize: Would I one day be infinitely sorrier for refusing to heed God's word than for having ignored Katherine? How much sorrier I might be when the full truth about human existence was revealed and I realized what a chance I had missed! It perplexed me to reflect how, in barely a week I had come to adopt a medieval outlook, accepting afterlife as a reality and salvation as the paramount purpose of our sojourn on earth.

I was now alert again, focused on what was going on. Another message was beginning to make itself felt. It was a number. At first I wasn't sure if it was 423 or 432, but gradually I settled on 432. There was a deliberate pause after the four, making me visualize it as 4:32, which I almost immediately concluded meant the time.

What was going to happen at 4:32 – whether to me or the world? Was I going to be struck down in some way, perhaps in an automobile accident or by something as ridiculous as slipping on the snow and breaking my neck? Or were the implications to be more universal, perhaps heralding the earthquake that would sink California beneath the waves of the Pacific or inundate the East Coast under a tidal wave surging over the top of the Empire State Building? In my condition, I wasn't ashamed to find relief in this abysmal thought, since a disaster of such magnitude would put me out of my misery as well. But almost instantly, I realized that because of the unredeemed state of my soul, I would merely be exchanging my temporal hell for an eternal one.

GET GOING, GET GOING . . .

As I continued to cower under the blankets, I had no doubt these messages would eventually make me crack; not in a way that would make me obey, but rather assure me a berth in a psychiatric ward. Since talking to my sister, the previous eve-ning on the phone, my condition had deteriorated. The reason was Al, the prayer leader whom I had called at Manya's behest. No, he didn't dispute or countermand what my sister said. If anything, he was more adamant that the messages were the devil's work and were to be ignored. I realized Al couldn't have possibly re-membered who I was. I had the feeling he visualized me as a teenager, intent on running away from home to join some devil-ish sect, and he considered it his duty to try to stop me or thwart my plans. "Jesus doesn't work that way," Al explained. "He wouldn't want you to run off halfcocked to who-knows-where and get your parents all upset . . . " As much as I appreciated this reassurance, Al's rationale had given him away. If there was one thing I remembered about Jesus Christ, it was his attitude on this point. Forget your family, Jesus had repeatedly urged, and follow me. I had checked it out myself before going to bed. There it was, spelled out in Saint Matthew. "A man's worst enemies will be the members of his family. Whoever loves his father or mother more than me is not worthy of me. Whoever does not take up his cross and follow in my steps is not worthy of me. Whoever tries to gain his own life will lose it." There! What could be more plain? This passage cast doubt on everything else Al and my sister had said. Their prescription of confession and communion no longer seemed a convincing substitute for what God had commanded me to do.

The occasional rattle of the radiator disrupted my thoughts and made me aware that the room was gradually heating up. I could smell the aroma of freshly brewed coffee wafting up from Mother's breakfast. God, how could I tell her I was leaving again? The stark images of what lay ahead once more invaded my brain. I could see myself working the night shift at the White Tower as a short order cook, when some glamorous people wander in after attending a charity play at an experimental theater nearby. Among them is the trendy shoe heiress from Saint Louis, who feared having to work in just such a place had she become my wife. Although I am a shadow of myself in a white T-shirt and a paper cap, she recognizes me right away, and nodding as if she understands, asks solicitously, "Are you all right?"

I tried to let my mind go blank. I didn't want to entertain these thoughts, or anything else pertaining to the reality closing in on me. I realized that my self-pitying act, coupled with my lack of determination and strength, was beginning to turn me into a self-parody.

"If you still want to leave," Father said, "go ahead. My God, you're over forty years old. Don't expect us to tell you what to do."

I could feel my innards tighten. My last buffer had crumpled. I was on my own.

Moments later, I was in my room. I normally never spent any time there during the day, but I had sneaked away from downstairs as soon as I discreetly could. Having that paper arrive at exactly 4:32, then finding the four-digit combination reprinted from the previous day, was making me lose all semblance of control.

I paced the little room back and forth, feeling as if my head might explode and splatter all over the place. Was this how Father had felt during his wartime drive to the Sudetenland with the prospect of having to share the stage with Henlein, the regional Nazi Gauleiter? To appear with this ruffian in what was to be a photo-op for the press would have been a betrayal of everything Father's family had symbolized for centuries. Yet an invitation from a Nazi of Henlein's rank was tantamount to a command, and to decline meant certain arrest, concentration camp and most likely death. Speeding along the narrow country road, Father crinkled his cheeks into a grimace that turned his eyes into slits. If only there were a way he could disappear, become invisible for a while, take temporary leave from this world – as I was so desperately praying for now! Just then Father saw a twelve-wheeled lumber truck roaring towards him on the opposite lane . . .

I pulled at my hair, then banged the palms of my hands against the sides of my head – hardly an admirable way to react even with nobody around. But that was my least worry now. I could already see eternal life and perfect knowledge floating out of my reach, as if I were on an iceberg inexorably drifting from shore, where basking in a golden light I could discern everything and everybody I loved, and they couldn't hear my cries for a final comforting glance. As I entered into the frigid darkness of this infinite void, how trifling seemed the years I might have to put in with the derelicts!

God no, spare me that train of thought! I hit my head against the wall several times in rhythmic raps, then sat down on the edge of my bed. This calmed me down, as if I had truly knocked some sense through my skull. I rubbed my face with my hands, then cradled my chin in my palms, elbows propped up against my knees. I realized I had little choice but to turn to the alternative my sister had proposed. Considering how inextricably trapped I felt, it didn't take me long to evolve a new rationale to validate Manya's approach. Wouldn't it be a blatant lack of faith in Jesus and his confessional, I reasoned, if I decided to go to skid row and personally tried to atone? Who was I to take matters into my hands and determine how much penance I should do? That was up to the Church, which was uniquely qualified to adjudge matters of this sort with its millennia of experience. Why, for all of my misdeeds and sins, they probably wouldn't sock me with more than several Our Fathers and a number of Hail Marys to match.

How trivial! I started to smirk, but suddenly was caught up in an infinitely greater truth that for the first time pierced the gloom which had enveloped me for days.

I sat up on the bed, electrified by what I now realized. How stupid and blind I was, how ignorant of God's mysterious ways! The answer had been there all along. All I had to do was to add up the facts. Here I was, ready to return to the Church after thirty years and partake in confession and communion, the most basic of all the sacraments. Had anyone suggested a week ago I would be thinking along these lines, I might have responded, though in jest, that only God could bring such a miracle about. Yet that's precisely what He had done! God obviously never intended for me to take him at his word about those Bowery derelicts. That had been His way of making me aware of the punishment He could demand and the mercy He could exercise. Nothing less than the trauma of the previous week could have gotten me to accept the Church and all that it entailed. Without those messages and various proofs, there is no way I would have taken such a step. Even if I had, how long would I have kept this commitment without the fearful memory of what I had been through? Yes, I would have to stick to the straight and narrow, yet how infinitely more welcome that would be than what I had faced! And I wouldn't be altogether weaseling out on the debt I still so acutely felt. I now remembered another near-providential fact. Just a few hundred yards from where I was going to live in Miami's Coconut Grove was Mercy Hospital. I could put in several hours each week with terminal indigents, and then during the summer months, perhaps volunteer a couple of weeks in camps for underprivileged youth. Yes, I was going to be starting a new life, liberated from the unwitting misorientation of my previous one.

Sitting at the edge of the bed, I felt suffused in a prayerful gratitude. *Oh, thank you God, thank you for being so persistent to make me see the light. You certainly work in astounding ways, and for a while, you sure gave me a scare. But thank you, God, for understanding me in your absolute wisdom and directing me in the only possible way. Nothing less extreme would have worked. You knew that all along. Now, I know it, too!*

111

15/

My sister arranged for me to confess the following day to a young charismatic priest not far from where she lived. Father Ted was his name, and Manya promised he would be understanding of my case.

"God does work in mysterious ways," she remarked joyfully, shortly after I arrived in the midst of a snow storm at her home and finished sharing with her my latest interpretation of God's intent. "I think you're absolutely right."

I couldn't resist reminding Manya of a crucial detail she seemed to be overlooking now. "But what if those messages had indeed come from the devil," I wanted to know, "as you and Al so confidently claimed? How could they have led to this providential result?"

My sister was hardly at a loss for words. "Well, the devil does overplay his hand every now and then," she said with a reassuring smile. "But I wouldn't give it another thought. Don't forget, Jesus was with you all the way, looking out for you and guiding you."

Manya left for the kitchen to phone Father Ted, while I remained seated on the living room couch. From the array of magazines on the coffee table at my feet, I picked up the first to catch my eye. It turned out to be a Catholic weekly, whose title I failed to notice in any memorable way. What did arrest my attention on about page three or five was a catchy ad for visiting the Holy Land. The tour was to be escorted by a priest named Father Carrigan, whose smiling, corpulent photo appeared above a headline: "THRILL to the Manger at Bethlehem! WEEP at the Via Dolorosa! CRUISE on the Sea of Galilee! CLIMB the Mount of Olives! ENJOY Cairo, Amman and Samaria!"

As I continued to peruse the ad, I had an empty feeling within. My God, it was no different from the enticing, mildly deceptive material I used to put out while working for the foreign study institute. In its implicit self-indulgence and fun, how reminiscent was this ad of the life to which I had heretofore subscribed! Maybe it wasn't by chance I came across this magazine now, any more than I had picked out seemingly at random the book by Thomas Merton. Maybe it was God himself who had intended for me to see Father Carrigan's ad and make me realize how far I was straying from my designated path. After all, what could Father Carrigan and his ilk have in common with the austere mission I had been called to carry out? Comfort was imprinted on his face, as well as on the faces of other priests pictured in prosperous social settings on the pages of this diocesan magazine.

As I continued to leaf through the glossy periodical, I started to get my anticlerical dander up. Hell no, I didn't want to have anything to do with this hierarchical institution, whose dogmas had the potential for inflicting discord and suffering. I couldn't help but feel hypocritical about my acceptance of the Christ story and the confessional to save my skin. What was I getting myself into? After all, I had never received any message from God to go to confession and communion. Was it really in the nature of God to resort to such devious ways? Perhaps all that deviousness had originated solely in my human brain . . .

Just then, my sister came bustling into the room. "Father Ted is waiting," she said, with an undertone of excitement. "He'll see you as soon as you can get there."

Outside the rectory, it was still snowing hard. The study where I found myself closeted with Father Ted was comfortable and warm. Several fresh logs were smoldering in the fireplace, quickly put there by an elderly domestic before she discreetly withdrew. Except for the sizable crucifix on one of the walls, this could have been a study or a den in any well-to-do New England home. Neat rows of books lined the other walls; there was an attractive carpet on the floor, and the furnishings had a rustic, antique look.

I felt curiously out of place. I came dressed as a penitent; as if I had, in fact, obeyed God's command and was on my way to skid row. I was wearing my battered sheepskin coat, my oldest Irish knit white sweater that was yellowing around the neck, and a pair of thick whipcord pants from one of my Saville Row suits I had taken out of commission years ago, after a dish of chicken tandoori at an Indian restaurant in London accidentally landed in my lap. As I now looked around, my guess was that most of the parishioners came here in their Sunday best. Shouldn't I at least tip off Father Ted to my sartorial disguise? I hadn't really meant to feign poverty, the way people often do when having their taxes audited. Perhaps if I were to let Father Ted know I usually wore custom made suits with four real buttonholes on each sleeve, he would be in a better position to visualize my sins. But it was just a fleeting thought. I figured my sins were overwhelming enough even in their attenuated form.

I liked Father Ted right away – and not only because he belied my stereotype of priests, which had just been reinforced by Manya's diocesan magazine. From the moment we met, Father Ted seemed to attune himself to my somber, remorseful mood. He was a thin, ascetic-looking man about ten years younger than I, who appeared impressed rather than overwhelmed by the worldly range of my sins. I must have been the classic case about which he had often preached but rarely encountered so full-blown in the flesh. During my two hours of often tearful outpouring, his attention never strayed as he listened with sympathy. I couldn't help but feel that my pathetically sorry state was validating for him the life of self-denial to which he had been called. He seemed almost surprised how readily the consequences of my freewheeling life confirmed the wisdom of the restricted path he advocated to his parishioners in church.

The only aspect of my outpourings that appeared to disturb Father Ted were my presumed communications with God. Normal people weren't supposed to have experiences of this sort unless, of course, proclaimed as saints or certified insane. With all of his church expertise, it wasn't anything Father Ted was prepared to comment on.

"The worst of it is, Father, I believe those communications more than what we're going through now."

"I don't think you'd be here if you didn't believe," he pointed out gently. "You believe enough to have come."

Maybe Father Ted was right, I tried to tell myself. Just to have driven here in the hazardous snow must have taken faith. Yet I felt I ought to be more forthright as to where I stood; to define the limits of my potential devotion – not unlike I had tried to do with that Fly Me! stewardess – prior to taking any irretrievable step. "What bothers me," I volunteered, as I shifted uneasily in my chair, "is that I don't really know to what extent I'm here as a substitute for what I was commanded to do."

"It's not unusual for human faith to begin when we're in dire need," Father Ted assured me, again showing no surprise at my admission. "This is how Jesus Christ brings us to him."

I managed a feeble smile. "I guess God knew how to whip me in line."

"This is only the first step, a chance for you to grow," Father Ted continued. "What's important is that you're sorry for your sins."

"I think that's embarrassingly obvious."

"Then I'm prepared to give you absolution."

I nodded uneasily. "Thank you, Father." My voice was subdued. Yes, of course, I wanted absolution. That's why I had come. Absolution gave Father Ted the power to do what no psychiatrist could. Instead of having to put me through extensive therapy to merely rationalize my sins, he had the authority to instantly wipe them out, thanks to a benefactor two thousand years ago.

Only I still couldn't quite get myself to believe that. My reservations were more fundamental than those I had shared with Father Ted. I wanted to shout that it wasn't the teachings of Jesus I objected to. It was the Church and the mumbo jumbo they had ritualized, including the confessional I was going through right now. I had often wondered what Christ would have thought of this Church which anathematized all other religions in his name.

Of course I didn't say any of this to Father Ted. Even in my distress, I retained sufficient PR savvy to know how far I could go. Father Ted would have had no choice but to withdraw his offer of absolution, at least until I had taken religious instructions to confirm my faith, a process that would probably have the opposite effect.

Father Ted began the prescribed rites, repeating whatever incantations were necessary to relieve me of my sins. He recognized how empty it would be to have me atone in any quantitative way; after all, how many prayers would I have to recite as a theoretical counterbalance for my sins? Seemingly unsure whether

I remembered any prayers at all, Father Ted asked me to pray silently with him. While he merely closed his eyes and remained in his chair as he started to recite quietly on my behalf, I tumbled to my knees, with tears streaming down my cheeks, as if to demonstrate my faith. Then during a pause in his supplications, I improvised a penitent prayer of my own, the likes of which I was sure Father Ted had never heard.

I was feeling increasingly grateful, as I continued to improvise my torrent of devotional words. It really was quite pleasant here, kneeling on the rug in this comfortable study protected from the outside snow, a crackling blaze in the fireplace. Was this why Jesus had died on the cross, so that people like me could be absolved in a matter of minutes for their years of transgressions? I had never considered the punishment to which I had been sentenced by God as excessive or unjust. But Jesus Christ, who had already suffered on my behalf, was making it unnecessary for me to serve any of that sentence at all.

When I paused momentarily in my prayerful outburst, Father Ted took the opportunity to punctuate my words with a brisk, *Amen!* I sensed that my outward zealotry was beginning to make him nervous. It obviously wouldn't be necessary for me to launch into any further spontaneous paeans.

"Thank you, Father Ted," I mumbled, getting back into my chair, grateful that this key requirement for salvation had been fulfilled. "I have one more favor to ask. I know it's supposed to be done only in conjunction with mass, but could you give me communion, too?"

Father Ted nodded. "I don't see why not. We'll just have to step next door to the church."

"I have to admit," I blurted out, "I was worried driving here in the snow. What if I had gotten killed before taking these sacraments? Would I have gone to hell?"

"The intent was there," Father Ted said calmly. He slipped on a pair of fur lined rubber boots and was bundling up against the snow. "God doesn't condemn people on a technicality."

His remark once more triggered my doubts.

A technicality! I thought to myself. Isn't that what I was going through right now, trying to circumvent what I had been so sternly commanded to do? Indeed, wasn't the underlying function of organized religion to provide a structure for helping us find acceptable ways of making up for our repeated failures to submit to God's will? Wasn't religious ritual our own compensation or offering to God, not unlike human, animal, and material sacrifices of the past, for not doing what he really wanted us to do?

Outside the rectory, gusts of wind whipped the heavy snow. Walking the few steps to the adjoining church through the gathering drifts, I found myself wishing I could take off my shoes and have the soles of my feet iced until discomfort became pain. Was that what may have partly motivated Emperor Henry IV a thousand years ago at the gates of the papal residence at Canossa, where he exposed himself to the winter cold for three days while waiting to be absolved? Was I really that different from him or, for that matter, from a shivering derelict I had seen several winters ago kneeling penitently with his last strength on the icy sidewalk amid the gaping, chic crowds of New York's Fifth Avenue?

There was a momentary delay. Father Ted had to clear the church of several acolytes, diligently practicing various aspects of the holy mysteries. They had the air of apprentice magicians or medical students at a hospital. The way they so quickly withdrew, with hushed whispers and furtive glances toward me, made me feel as if they were yielding to some grave emergency.

Father Ted started his incantations. As I knelt uncertainly before him at the altar, I kept reminding myself of his words that I wouldn't be here if I didn't believe. Yet, awaiting the thin wafer that had supposedly been transubstantiated into the body of Christ, I was racked with the most intense doubts so far. Was this perhaps my ultimate hypocrisy? Wasn't I entering into as much of an ironclad commitment for the rest of my days as if I had gone to work with the Bowery derelicts? How long would I be able to carry out my church-imposed obligations and chores? Perhaps God had understood me more completely than I thought. Perhaps I would have been able to adjust better had I submitted directly to His will rather than opting for the prerequisites of the Church. I might even have unexpectedly fallen in love in a strange and exciting way with that skid row ordeal.

But I had made my choice. As I now felt the wafer on my tongue, I kept repeating to myself it was Jesus Christ who was entering my body, fervently hoping I might again have that exultant feeling I had experienced at the prayer meeting conducted by Al. What a wonderful bond it would be for this shotgun marriage! It would prove I wasn't an opportunist and a fraud; that I wasn't resorting to this union merely for security and out of fear. *Please Jesus, give me that feeling now . . . yes, now!*

But that feeling never came.

119

16/

I continued to carry out my obligatory chores, having already gone to mass two Sundays in a row. I even lined up with other parishioners to receive communion on both occasions, which I didn't have to do. But I wanted to show my good faith. As I inched closer to the altar, where the tasteless little wafer was placed on my tongue, I tried to reassure myself that this was, in fact, the body of Christ. I still remembered as a six-year-old, living in a little village away from Prague during the war, being strictly warned by the old priest preparing our class for first communion, never, never to bite the wafer, but to let it slowly dissolve in my mouth. Otherwise, it might suddenly spurt blood, since what we would be biting or poking would be the body of Christ. Although none of us boys had dared put that theory to a test, I was tempted to do so now. What more convincing proof to resolve my doubts? But as I now saw other parishioners that had been ahead of me in line openly and without undue concern chewing on theirs, I realized it wouldn't work. The rules must have changed, or this one had never been in force except with that old village priest.

I didn't mind so much going to church as I did the idea of feeling coerced by means of not too subtle threats. To think that for the rest of my days I would have to go; not only on Sundays, but on holy days of obligation too, or risk committing a mortal sin. As Manya had apprised me not so long ago, only one of those was sufficient to put me back in the peril of hell. In such a case, I could only hope not to die before having a chance to cleanse myself anew through the Church's sacraments – coupled, of course, with a sincere resolve not to miss mass again.

I also felt embarrassed how others might perceive my new life, perhaps more so than by any misdeed or aberration that could have been dredged up from my past. Being a fearful, lockstep churchgoer was an image grotesquely at odds with the one I had cultivated for years. How could I explain my behavior to friends, as their frequent guest at sumptuous country homes? I was the one they usually relied on to keep other guests entertained in a light, upbeat mood. For me to interrupt a leisurely Sunday brunch or a few sets of tennis to go to mass might cast a pall over everyone there, as if exposed to some contagious disease. My situation was harder to explain than lugging along a pressure cooker and supply of zucchini, as I had done for nearly two years while being faithful to Dr. Bieler's regimen. About that, my friends had at least been able to joke.

I was already having a problem at home. Again, not so much with Father, who was focused on his daily physical routines that kept him in buoyant health and helped him sell his exercise machines. When he noticed that attending mass had become part of my Sunday program, he shrugged it off as an expected aberration of a rootless bachelor of my age. "Thank God," he remarked several times subsequent to my session with Father Ted, "at least you've come back to your senses." Mother, however, interpreted my churchgoing as a continuation of an ominous pattern. It was as sure an indication I hadn't recovered from my malady as if I were still running a low-grade fever. She worried and fretted that my condition could suddenly flare up with its former distressing symptoms. That's why I was glad I would be driving to Florida soon. At least there I would have a place of my own. Even having to face that Fly me! stewardess two doors down would be easier to finesse than Mother's constantly scrutinizing gaze.

Ah yes, what was I to do about sex, now that I was beginning to feel a diminution of that acute premonition of having forever forfeited my chances of having a family. At my age, it was logical that maybe a childless relationship is what I was going to have to settle for, much to my father's distress. And while I still wasn't interested in resuming this more limited quest, the mere thought of having to subscribe to the Church's teachings in this area depressed me more than anything else.

Despite this tendency to make a scapegoat of the Church, I had to face the facts. I could no more blame the Church for my depression than I could have blamed Dr. Bieler years ago for the breakdown in my health. I felt no less grateful to Father Ted than to any doctor who had treated me in the past. Father Ted couldn't have been more effective had he prescribed the latest wonder drug against the disorder I had. I was still so intimidated by those messages that I felt the need to go to church without any doctrinal imperatives or threats of mortal sins. That's why I was continuing to go to communion as well; to assuage my sorrow for having sinned and perhaps mollify God's wrath. I felt a need to remind myself of the true enormity of my transgressions and use them as a baseline from which to improve. If the Church hadn't been there, I would have had to invent some reasonable facsimile. I even found the ritual of mass comforting. The only part to which I took exception was the communal affirmation of faith: having to stand with the rest of the flock and proclaim my exclusive belief in the One Holy, Catholic, Apostolic Church. But by the second Sunday, I learned to anticipate this unacceptable oath in time to mentally stuff up my ears.

The harshest fact I had to face didn't relate to any doctrine of the Church. It simply was that my approach to life had failed. Aside from any fears of damnation in some hypothetical ethereal world, my behavior had sabotaged my best interests here on earth. By allowing the pursuit of immediate pleasure to dominate my life, I had harbored an unseen enemy. To think what I had endured in the guise of my romantic quest by just catering to the most demanding part of my physical self! Yet that arousable appendage had merely been acting in concert with the far larger body of which it was a part. Motivated primarily by the prolongation or repetition of what seemed most pleasurable at the moment, this physical self routinely imposed ultimatums on my behavior irrespective of broader considerations or interests. My whole life had been subservient to that seductive goal; my actions repeatedly distorted, the promises of pleasure driving me to do things I wouldn't otherwise have deigned to do. I always felt obliged to keep my options open in case still greater pleasures beckoned, whether to visit some fabulous new place or to woo a potential bride of unprecedented appeal.

And where did all that get me?

Clearly, I would have to change my act, if only to find some semblance of happiness in everyday life. Even without the restrictions imposed by the Church, I would need to adopt a new modus operandi. I could just as easily have drawn on the precepts formulated some twenty-five hundred years ago by Gautama Buddha. How well I understood the Buddha's fundamental premise that our craving for pleasure was the cause of earthly suffering! He had at one time sounded to me like a loon; and, if I were to go out in the street and repeat to the first dozen people I met his conclusions, they would regard me as equally wacky. Yet, how valid were the Buddha's words! – no doubt, far more applicable in our opulent times than in his day.

Alas, how truly limited we were! Maybe only the meekest among us were able to safely negotiate our magnificent pathways, where on every corner lurked some tempting indulgence or delight. Was that the meaning of the Biblical promise that the meek would inherit the Earth – and Heaven, too? Perhaps humanity still was no different from Adam and Eve, and eating from the forbidden tree no less perilous – to each of us individually, and when multiplied millions and millions of times, on a global scale as well. Whatever paradise we had so painstakingly built on earth could be lost in a trice.

PART TWO
1979 - 1983

1/

It was the end of January by the time I felt rational enough to leave home for the drive south, reasonably certain I wouldn't see God materialize on I-95 to block my way somewhere between North and South Carolina.

"Everything will work out for you just fine," Father assured me jovially, as he was preparing for an early start to his Exercycle office in Boston. "Maybe now you'll even write something interesting. Before, you were too normal." He picked up a copy of *The New York Times*, which he would later prop up on the car's steering wheel and glance at when traffic on the Mass Pike wasn't too heavy.

Mother looked glum, as she walked me to the car in the snow-covered driveway. Hunched over and all bundled up with a heavy scarf wrapped around her head, she looked like a Russian grandmother from one of Tolstoy's villages. "Don't ever tell anyone what happened to you here," she admonished, with a worried mien that nevertheless conveyed the warmth of her love. "They would have to think the same as I."

That was the least of my concerns. As I pulled out of the driveway, my mind was in a turmoil from having already caught myself backsliding from my resolve. In packing my belongings for the new apartment in Coconut Grove, I had filled my little hatchback car to the roof, leaving no room to pick up some shivering hitchhiker along the way. Although I off-loaded enough before starting out to free up the front seat – including those etchings of my ancestors I had vowed not to take – this didn't spare me from tormenting myself as I headed south. Wasn't what had just occurred ample proof I was resuming my former ways? Was that why God had so implacably insisted on dedicating my life to the derelicts and making the seemingly cruel break with my past? Was that the only way to truly change as required for salvation? I found myself drawing an unholy parallel with old Dr. Bieler's words, *You'll get well, if you're careful!* Had Dr. Bieler been so rigid about his unpalatable diet because he knew that any pleasurable deviation would inevitably escalate? That an occasional sliver of cake or a glass of wine would eventually lead to indulging in haute French cuisine?

What may have saved me from an accident while in this frame of mind was that I stopped for the night at my older brother's house in Philadelphia. A corporate lawyer and partner of one of the country's highly respected firms, he understood the meaning of stress. He recognized my symptoms, and shortly before going to bed, handed me one of his Dalmane sleeping pills. "Don't argue, just take it," he said in the same tone he had used to boss me around in our youth.

It was the best sleep I'd had since this endless nightmare began. The next morning, I was still feeling pleasantly tranquilized – and remained that way for the rest of the fifteen-hundred-mile drive. Even in this mildly stupefied condition, I was able to concentrate on the road better than if I had remained in my alert but agitated state. And tucked in my pocket was a small vial of those magic pills, which my brother had pressed on me as I was about to leave. Practical considerations at this stage took precedence over any lingering worries about blunting my potential to receive further messages.

As soon as I arrived in Miami, I began working on the daycare scripts. I had originally signed the contract reluctantly through a seeming mental lapse. The daycare centers were for children primarily from deprived families and could hardly have provided the milieu to which I was partial at that time. Had God tipped my hand way back then, knowing how I would welcome this work now?

By the end of the week, I was also reporting to volunteer at Mercy Hospital, which was so significantly close to my apartment in Coconut Grove. Hoping to approximate my original calling, I asked to work with terminal indigents who had nobody else in the world. My first assignment was at a nursing home, where the hospital warehoused cases of this sort. A glance down one of the bathroom-tiled corridors and a whiff of the stale urine smell confirmed the horror stories about places of this sort. Wherever I looked, I could see seemingly abandoned wheelchairs containing aged human flesh with vacuous eyes, sporadically groaning and aimlessly reaching out.

The one exception was ninety-three-year-old Fred. Though in a near-mummified state, he retained an optimistic gleam. "I don't know how old I am," he observed, as if pleasantly baffled, sitting in his cranked-up bed. "I think I must be at least fifty. They keep telling me here I'm sixty. I don't think I am. I was one of ten children, you know? My mother cooked for us, and it was excellent. Other mothers, maybe they also cook good. But our mother, she cooked really excellent . . . You know, I am one of ten children. I don't know how old I am. I must be at least sixty. They keep telling me I'm only fifty. . . "

Old Fred was obviously feeling no pain. Besides, he already had visitors, a solicitous niece accompanied by her grumpy but understanding spouse.

I was politely bowing out when I spotted the type of case I had in mind. He was the other occupant of the room, stretched out on a bed at the foot of Fred's. He looked terribly alone, as he lay there fully clothed, eyes open, staring blankly into space. That he didn't seem especially old and had no visible ailment made his condition all the more compelling.

"How are you?" I asked, as jovially as I could.

"Rotten," he said, with deadly gloom.

"You'll get better."

"No, I won't. And I don't care."

"Is there anything you need?"

"Don't bother, doc. It ain't worth it."

"Does anybody come to see you?"

"No, nobody comes to see me. My wife died eighteen years ago." He glanced at Fred across the room, then eyed me carefully. "Are you a relative of Fred's?"

"No, no. I just stopped by to say hello."

"Well, I say it because you look a lot like Fred."

"Do you talk much to Fred?"

"Naw, nothing much worth talking about."

There was a pause. I walked around to the foot of the bed and looked at his medical chart. "I see your name is Mr. Brady."

"Yeah, Phil Brady."

"Well, you're going to be just fine, Phil. I'll come back to see you again soon."

"Whatever you say, doc."

"You're sure there isn't anything I can bring?"

Phil seemed hesitant, then shook his head. "Naw, I don't want to be no trouble."

"It won't be, really it won't."

"Well, I always liked tangerines. They don't give you none here. But as I said, I don't want to be no trouble."

A couple of days later I was back, a brown paper bag of tangerines in hand. I again found Phil fully dressed in bed, staring off into space. But he seemed to have taken a turn for the worse. He was deep under the covers, and despite the fetid mugginess in the room, he was shivering and looked fearfully withdrawn.

"How are you, Phil?" I asked with evident concern.

"Oh God," he moaned, trying to burrow deeper under the covers. "You'd have to see me this way!"

"Is there anything I can do?"

"Would you please get out? Can't you see, I don't want to be bothered!"

I stood there, stung by the venom of his words.

"And don't come back no more!"

I felt flushed, as if hit on the nose. I deposited the bag of tangerines on a chair by Phil's bed and beat a hasty retreat.

Driving home, I was struggling to control my pride. Was this my reward for having gone to all this trouble on his behalf? I quickly had to remind myself: I wasn't doing this for fun and praise. How easy it would be to take Phil at his word, a handy excuse never to return. But I knew he had acted this way because he was depressed. Yes, I would try again, I repeated to myself. And again and again until I was able to get through to Phil and help him in some way, if only with another bag of tangerines.

By the time I returned home, I had forgotten the harshness of Phil's words. I was feeling a new resolve, a buoyancy of spirit that came from sensing that I was on the right path.

2/

My sojourn in Miami didn't consist entirely of ministering to terminal indigents. I did that only as much as I had promised – no more than several hours a week. Neither did I go to church beyond Sundays and holy days of obligation, though I did attend Wednesday evening prayer meetings of a nearby charismatic group that Manya had tracked down through her network of religious friends. Some in the group seemed blithely carefree, filled with a consuming joy they said they felt from having Jesus at their side, walking with them through life. Especially Sol, whom I first spotted among this shirt-sleeved group because of his custom-made suits with four button holes on each sleeve. This elegant, sixty-year-old Jewish businessman born in Minsk unabashedly explained during one meeting how he had lost his Miami-based multimillion-dollar plastics business, and coming out of a three-day drunk with a prostitute, was bent on suicide. He was about to gulp down several hundred aspirins after the pistol he had with him failed to work, when he suddenly felt Christ's comforting grace. It seemed to descend on him spontaneously, with no prodding on his part, although it may have come through the influence of his equally elegant Cuban wife. She had been praying for years that Sol would stop his gallivanting and be converted to Christ. Now, she felt a trifle miffed to see her husband vaulted to a plane beyond hers. "I did all the praying, and he gets all the grace," I heard her say with a sigh. Composing his poems to Christ, Sol appeared to be traipsing in a heavenly world. Week after week I saw him filled with the same carefree joy, whether working as a night watchman at a warehouse or negotiating trades in truckloads of plastic scraps. As he gradually returned to affluence, nothing mattered to Sol provided he felt Christ was at his side. Of course, there were others in that prayer group who looked depressed as if hopelessly mired in life. I could understand how the praying and singing and the pervasive communal spirit soothed the internal anguish they felt. That's why I also went – and to see my friend Sol.

Otherwise I led a fairly normal life. I worked on the daycare center scripts and socialized in a subdued way with my younger brother, Tom, who had a little house on North Miami Beach and worked as a cameraman-director for advertising spots and documentaries. I had given him his start in the business by hiring him years ago for the Institute's publicity film, before he had ever held a camera in his hand. We had a warm, easy relationship and these visits had a calming effect on my restive psyche.

I was anxious to remain vigilant against any and all licentious thoughts. That Fly Me! stewardess two doors down was no temptation at all, although I did make various gestures at merely being friends, which she frostily rebuffed. The most formidable threat I faced was on the beach, where I spent a couple of hours each day, if only to stay in shape and keep my brain alert. It was an ordeal to rivet my eyes straight ahead, as if I had blinders on – even to cup my hands along the sides of my face to keep my vision from straying right and left, and God forbid, come to rest between some pretty girl's legs. I realized how an East Block Communist must have felt on being exposed to the consumer goods in our capitalist world. If I unavoidably did glimpse an especially alluring female part – a pretty rear, a shining mane of hair – I was determined not to break my stride, though I might be passing up the most beautiful woman in the world. I tried to rationalize that if I backtracked to double-check, the rear might belong to a not so attractive face, and the shining mane to a not so attractive rear. Yet, it was precisely this sort of checking out I would have to learn to avoid; to stop reducing human personalities and lives to such superficial once-overs. Considering my past, this was a monumental task; in effect, a do-it-yourself deprogramming course. But whenever I managed to hold firm, I ended up with a sense of victory over my baser self. And if I happened to overcome several temptations in a row, I would feel a surge of confidence that promised to make the next temptation easier to surmount.

It nevertheless remained a struggle not to succumb, not to sneak more than an occasional peek out of the corner of my eye day after day. And I made it through several months relatively unscathed, having necked only once with another resident in the apartment complex, and very briefly at that. What terminated that relationship was when I tried to confide to her the details of the ethereal experience from which I had so recently emerged. She shrank from me as if I were a dangerous crank.

Then I had an accident of sorts, probably because I had relaxed my guard. Having already decided to move to Laguna Beach as soon as I finished the daycare scripts, the remaining weeks in Coconut Grove were hardly adequate to initiate a lasting liaison, and God forbid I should consider anything else.

She seemed to materialize out of nowhere; a buxom twenty-year-old radiating an enticing smile as she approached me with a civic minded petition to sign. I was impressed that already at her age, she was volunteering so selflessly. Nor could I completely ignore the way she fit into her short-short cut-off dungarees, and how her knit polo shirt displayed her athletic build.

My ostensible intent was to play Cupid, to talk to her on behalf of my younger brother, who was out of town on a film shoot for several days. Although Tom had an astonishing supply of candidates in his own search for the ideal bride, he wasn't likely to turn down additional interviewees.

Yet she somehow ended up at my place. Her name was Sallie, and she had her heart set on a career in costume design. She appeared to be exceptionally intelligent and slightly crude in an exciting way. She was from a suburb of Peoria, Illinois, where her parents owned a third-generation haberdashery, and Sallie had for a time carried on with the local fire chief. Now, just the way she positioned herself on the couch made me realize I was in for a siege. The more I tried to shrink away and protest, the more aggressive she became. "You sure play harder to get than my man back home," she laughed, deftly negotiating the buttons on the front of my shirt. "He had the same cute silvery hairs on his chest, but you're in better shape, and he was married."

"How about my brother?" I reminded her.

She ran her hand down to my waist. "How do I know I'll even like him?"

"He's younger and better looking."

"You're good enough for . . . "

"But I told you, I'm leaving in a few weeks."

"That gives us lots of time."

I was beginning to experience the mixed feelings of an alcoholic confronted with a drink. She had somehow managed to get me to stretch out on the couch and was squeezing herself next to my extended form. "I promise I won't do anything you don't want me to," I heard her mutter in a strangely reminiscent way, as if borrowing a line from my past. "Let me just lie here next to you."

For a moment, she kept her word. But just then, I felt her slip out of her clothes, and most deftly disencumber me of my own. My God, I moaned, how did I get into this? I could already feel her moist warmth, and before I knew it, it was too late. God no, no! I tried to protest as she reassured me with another line I recognized so well: "Why not slip it in just a little," she whispered. "I promise, if you don't like it, you can take it out."

This incident confirmed what I had already suspected: there was no such thing as being careful enough. Only if I had gone to work with the Bowery derelicts would I have been safe. Not that I had anything against the physical aspects of what Sallie put me through. It was the lingering psychological trauma of this casual onetime encounter I couldn't countenance, an unpleasant feeling deep within as if I had mangled or torn something that was meant to remain whole. Was this the result of trying to uncouple a momentary pleasure from what had been coupled over eons of human evolution by nature, if not by the hand of God?

One of the aftereffects of that carnal tumble was to rededicate myself to volunteer efforts. The case I was assigned when I showed up at the hospital's volunteer office involved an outpatient, 75-year-old Nikos, whom I first met in the nephrology ward. Reclining in a contraption similar to a dentist's chair, he was covered to his chest with a white sheet, and from a permanently implanted shunt in his arm that bulged like a huge vein, his blood circulated through clear plastic tubing into a whirring dialysis machine.

Nikos was a tall, emaciated, olive-skinned former short order cook born in Greece. He had labored his whole life, often twelve hours a day, and once went for three years without a Sunday off. The reason he was destitute was because of his wife, a homely, rotund woman whose tinted photo in an antique silver frame Nikos carried wherever he went. It took the entire seventeen thousand dollars he had saved from his lifetime of work to keep his wife alive a few extra weeks after she had been diagnosed with terminal cancer of the brain.

"And I'm grateful for every day," Nikos unhesitatingly told me, as I helped him mow the lawn behind the neat little house he owned in a marginal neighborhood of similar homes. "We had been married for thirty-five years. She knew me so well. After I retired, I liked to go fishing. I'd lose track of time and come home a couple of hours late. Ever so gently, she would shout, 'Where were you this time, you tramp?' And I'd say, 'Did you miss me, you hag?' Oh, we had such fun."

Of my various charges, Nikos alone questioned the motives for my work. "The first time I see you," he confided, as soon as he began to feel comfortable with me, "I say to myself, hey wait a minute, what's this guy doing here? I mean, you were dressed so elegant. Why would someone like him be wanting to waste time on someone like me? He must be troubled or something. There must be more to it than meets the eye." Nikos shook his head. "And you shouldn't be wasting your time on me. You should be married, have a family, find a partner for life . . ."

Nikos seemed to appreciate my visits but became vague whenever I suggested a date to see him again. "I can't promise anything," he would say. "It's better if you call first." I knew he refused to contact his only son, an executive with an electronics firm in Texas, whom he had sent to college on his minimum wage. "He's got a family of his own," Nikos quietly explained. "I don't want to bother him. He has enough worries already." As calm as Nikos remained, I knew how much it hurt to have been abandoned by his own flesh and blood.

Nikos's one regret was that he had never made it back to the fishing village in Greece where he had been born. "I was eight when I come to America. I have four brothers and five sisters still live there. For each sister I sent money for her wedding. All my life I hope to see them once more. My two eyes next to their two eyes, understand? Then my wife, she get sick." Nikos glanced at the small tinted photo in the silvery frame propped up on the kitchen table where we were sitting. "And I don't regret it, not one cent. She deserve every penny." Nikos rubbed his face, then looked at me intently across the Formica table top. "Oh, you're so lucky! You've been everywhere. You've done everything. You've seen everything. Me? I spent my whole life with pots and pans and cook hamburgers to go. Oh, you don't know how very lucky you are!"

I sat there, uncertain what to say. Nikos had just congratulated me for having experienced a thousand times my share of pleasure in life – exactly as I used to congratulate myself.

Nikos seemed to read my mind. "When you die, you go to sleep. There's nothing. No heaven, no hell. I remember in the little village in the old country where I grew up, when there was a rainbow, the old women said, 'God is happy.' Lightning and thunder, 'God is mad.' I have no education. I leave school after five years. But I read. All the time, read, read, read. I know about the Inquisition. I know about the Reformation. Nobody agree on anything and everybody say, 'I am right.' What is religion? I'll tell you what it is: Be good! I don't have to give you my shoes. But if your feet are cold, maybe I have an extra pair of socks."

I could see Nikos growing progressively weak. "I think they're taking too much water out of my blood," he explained, unable to keep up alongside of me as I slowly mowed his lawn. "You may think I'm crazy, but you know my pigeon Taki? A few weeks before my wife die, he start to bite her like crazy. He never bite me before. Lately, he's been at me pretty steady. But that's all right."

I wasn't surprised a couple of weeks later to reach a recorded disconnect message on Nikos's phone. It was just like him to want to go quietly, not to be any bother.

3/

My stay in the Coconut Grove apartment was drawing to a close. I had finished those daycare center scripts, and management was eager to release me from my lease. They had a waiting list and wanted to raise the rent. Eight months had passed since that searing conflagration at my parents' home, for which I had no explanation yet. Some days had been better than others; a few, much worse. That's when the flames would suddenly flare and remind me of the burning question that remained: was it really God who had singed my soul? I had yet to come across anyone who had heard of a similar case. Was I some sort of a loon, destined never to know the truth?

All in all, I thought I was handling the problem well. From the dozen or so sleeping pills my older brother had given me, I still had several left. I was also benefiting from having discovered how to use coffee as a euphoric drug. The secret was to drink it no more than once a week. A five-hundred milligram jolt would then provide more of a rise than I imagined any amphetamine could; especially when taken in an aesthetic dosage form, a triple sized broad-rimmed cup of Limoges porcelain, hand-painted in France. A couple of sluggish withdrawal days would invariably follow; perhaps a low-grade headache, a touch more depression than at other times. But that was a price I was prepared to pay for an exhilarating day that reminded me how I used to feel, which helped carry me through until another fix the following week.

I didn't go directly to Laguna Beach. One of the celebrated producers of Imax documentary films in New York, Francis Thompson, commissioned me to do a short script for Southern Railroad. This would add several thousand dollars to my freedom buffer in the bank, and enable me to visit my sister and parents in Massachusetts. Mother had looked so glum when she waved me good-bye, and I wanted to take this opportunity to reassure her about my mental state. I also wanted to pick up some of those etchings of my ancestors I had left behind, including the one of a bemedaled field marshal, my great grandfather, whose gently sloping forehead and distinctive nose both my Father and I shared. I had missed having them on my apartment walls in Florida, and I no longer saw anything wrong with taking them out West. Surely, Father Ted would have said they were no peril to my soul.

While working on the railroad script in New York, I ran into that statuesque stockbroker, Annette, who had sent me off with her verdict that I should wear a sandwich board, warning unsuspecting girls I was a fraud. This time it was Annette who had spotted me in the street and hugged me like a dear old friend. She was eager to let me know that she was happily married to a real estate developer, and before we parted invited me to join her and her husband for dinner at their Manhattan coop.

That evening over cocktails Annette confided she was shocked how depressed I looked. "You should be out there doing your thing, picking up girls and having fun!" she exclaimed after several glasses of wine, as the three of us sat down to eat. "That would blow away the little cloud I see hovering over your head. Remember, we have a right to be happy."

"Yes, but maybe not the way everyone tells us to."

"I think you're missing out on life."

When I tried to explain during the meal some of what I had been through, Annette nodded sympathetically but kept coming back to the same theme. "You need to cheer up, to be your old self," she observed in a well-meaning way. "If you're a little out of touch, I'm sure I could find one or two of my friends who'd be glad to help. I promise, you won't have to marry them. How long did you say you're staying?"

Remembering how Annette had wailed about my irresponsible ways, I couldn't help but smile. She had at that time urged me to see a psychiatrist to set me straight; now she seemed genuinely concerned I wasn't having non-committal fun. When I tried to point this out, she affectionately grasped my hand. "Ah, but you weren't happy then, either."

"I don't think I'll solve anything by regressing."

She smiled. "But you were happier."

"My view of happiness is changing."

"That's why you should see a therapist." She glanced at her husband. "Ours is terrific. We've been seeing her . . . well, since before we got married. She could really help."

"I don't want to waste the money," I said.

She shook her head. "I think you're afraid of the truth."

"I would welcome the truth. Believe me, it would be a relief."

"Then why don't you see her?"

"What can she tell me that I haven't figured out on my own? As for the rest, the messages, Blackie, God . . ." I shrugged helplessly.

Annette remained unconvinced. "I still think you're afraid to find out."

The therapist turned out to be an attractive, well-groomed woman of youthful middle age. Her office was in the same building off Park Avenue as Big Stick Beneventi's, the urologist known for his agonizing treatments with a J-shaped rod, whom I had frequented a dozen years ago following an unfortunate tumble with an especially endearing editorial assistant.

The therapist took copious notes while I tried to convey to her the salient points of my case. I didn't feel the same desire to unburden myself as I had with Father Ted, but the realization that I was paying more than a dollar-a-minute [in 1980!] made me no less forthcoming. Whenever I mentioned God, she nodded significantly, as if I wasn't completely sane. And she seemed to regard the details of my sexual restraint as gravely as if I were an anorexic refusing to eat.

"Do I understand it correctly," she interjected in an artificially detached way, "you don't now masturbate?"

"Only when absolutely necessary," I explained. "Usually no more than once a week."

"Do you think you're depressed?"

"Obviously, I'm not elated, but I really don't mind," I said, unable to resist launching into a broader perspective. "If the ancient Greeks were right that from suffering comes wisdom, maybe I'll become moderately wise."

"I see," the therapist said, as if I were further confirming that I was mentally unwell.

"Surely, Aeschylus wasn't demented," I persisted, "but merely insightful into our human lot. That's why his dramas are as fresh today as twenty-five hundred years ago."

This observation drew a momentary blank. But in the next instant the therapist regained her aplomb and gave me a patronizing smile. "Don't you think you're being a little hard on yourself?"

The hackneyed query made me laugh. "The last thing I need is help in rationalizing away my misdeeds."

"Remember, you have a right to be happy," she countered with the phrase I recognized that Annette had used.

"Unfortunately, that's a recent assumption. Maybe it's no coincidence our civilization seems to be collapsing."

She pursed her lips and shook her head as she busied herself making more notes, while glancing not so discreetly at her watch. She charged me seventy-five dollars and had no qualms in expressing her preference to be paid right away. Later, she confided to Annette over the phone that on a scale of one to ten — ten being suicidal and requiring immediate hospitalization — I was a solid eight, possibly a nine. What if the therapist had seen me several months earlier in the midst of my divine throes?

"She's convinced she can help," Annette announced, when I visited her again to say good bye. "If you ask me, I think you should stay right here in New York. Get a job you can handle easily. I mean in your condition. Selling books at Brentano's or something. That will keep you occupied and give you enough to live on modestly. You can use the money you've set aside for California to see her at least twice a week. She has a special long-term rate. You'd normally be eligible after several months, but I think I could talk her into giving it to you from the start."

God, I would really have to be insane to do that; to totally disorient my life to help this unremarkable therapist fill her appointment book. It would make far less sense than if I had gone to work with the derelicts in the first place.

"It's too late to change my plans," I told Annette, who I knew had my best interests at heart. "I can't wait to get out to California. You know how I've always talked about Laguna Beach."

"Then promise me," she said with heartfelt concern, "you'll find a therapist the minute you get there."

I sort of nodded, just as I did a week later when I briefly saw my sister Manya, and she urged me with equal concern to find a charismatic prayer group.

It was the only way, they both had said.

4/

In Laguna Beach, I found almost right away what I was looking for – a tiny, furnished A-frame house that was indefinitely for rent. Perched on a rocky bluff some sixty feet above a little crescent beach, this one-room dwelling was only a few hundred yards from the more sumptuous quarters I had occupied a decade earlier while undergoing Dr. Bieler's cure of a debilitating condition he called starch toxemia. I hoped to be no less successful in finding an answer for whatever was disturbing me now.

Within a month in this exotic place, I was settled into a routine that included attending a weekly mass at a nearby Catholic church. Though I had yet to make an effort to connect with a charismatic group or find a psychiatrist, I was about to see a doctor of a different stripe. He had been my classmate for four years at that Connecticut boarding school and now was a prominent surgeon on the West Coast. Known affectionately as Buzzy by his close friends, Francis G. had been a scholarship boy like me. Although one of the big wheels in our class, whereas I had started out as one of the smallest boys, he had always been friendly in returning my greetings in the corridors. I hadn't seen him since graduation, but when I chanced in the local bookstore on a thoughtful collection of poetry he had published through a San Diego press, I called the alumni office for his address. I was delighted to learn he lived in LaJolla, just an hour's drive down the coast.

Francis greeted me by the arched, double front door of his sprawling, Spanish-style hillside home. He had obviously done well. Starting with the same advantages as I, he appeared to be yet another example of how far I had fallen behind. The years had also been kind to Francis physically. He still had the type of tall, pretty boy looks other men often resent and women adore. Wearing jeans and no shoes, he was relaxed and tanned as if he no longer worked. He was the one who had suggested on the phone that we meet in midmorning of a weekday and take a long walk together. He seemed in no rush as he introduced me to his wife and showed me through his tastefully furnished house, pausing in front of the photos of two modish, college-age students. Our tour ended by the pool, where I was astounded to see a five-meter diving board. Francis explained he had installed it several years ago for his son, who was then on the Colgate College diving team and had hopes of making the Olympics. "Didn't quite make it," my host concluded, "but he still uses it when he visits." By the time Francis finally suggested we start our walk,

I was again wondering: was this the schedule of one of the most prominent surgeons in the state?

Trekking along a narrow trail on a rocky bluff high above La-Jolla's shore, we exchanged pleasantries at first; which classmates each of us had seen, who was where and doing what. I had been preparing to question Francis about some of the more challenging aspects of his lifesaving role as a surgeon. But then in no time at all, and without deliberately intending to do so, I found myself broaching the subject of my traumatic rebuke by God. I felt an immediate trust for this contemporary of mine, as if the schoolboy experience we had shared predisposed him to understand. I had never come forth so readily with anyone except Father Ted (to whom I had since sent a hundred-dollar check) and that New York shrink, who had the clock running.

Francis appeared intent on hearing me out, as he walked a step ahead on the rugged coastal path winding through heavy brush and past several eucalyptus trees. "That voiceless source sounded just like the Duke at his terrifying best," I said, in a lighthearted reference to our school's storied headmaster.

My companion abruptly stopped. We had reached a clearing high on a bluff, and I thought he wanted to rhapsodize over the expansive ocean view. Instead, he turned to face me. "You won't believe this," he said, with a faint smile. "You're the second person to come to me this month. Just last week, a friend I hadn't seen in fifteen years called from Pittsburgh and insisted on flying here to talk. I must have listened to a half-dozen people in the past several years. The details are different, but the gist of what they're so anxious to share is the same." Francis's disarming smile broadened. "You know, already when you phoned the other day I had a feeling this is what you wanted to talk about."

My heart perked up. He sounded like Dr. Bieler telling me he had diagnosed my ailment the moment I walked into his San Juan Capistrano office. Maybe it wasn't entirely by chance I had come across this former classmate's little book of poetry, and that he happened to live so near.

"You could say these experiences reflect a form of borderline schizophrenia," he explained. "That, of course, doesn't make them any less real. The strange dimension or reality was there all along. You and the others just needed to be in a special frame of mind to perceive it."

"I sure was perceiving more than I wanted to," I said, eager to provide my doctor-friend with more details. "You'll probably think me completely loco, but I had a compulsion to give up everything and go off to the Bowery. I wanted to dedicate the rest of my life to helping derelicts and drunks. I know it sounds crazy, a guilt neurosis or whatever . . . "

Francis was now signaling with an upraised arm to let him speak. "That appears to be the common factor. A seemingly irrational drive to do something you absolutely don't want to do, and your better judgment warns you against. It can be as trivial as crossing a street at a certain point or as critical as breaking with your past. It's only after you have given in to it that bingo, you're free. You no longer feel you have to do it."

I stood there astonished. I hadn't said a word about how I had put away that dinner only to be told I could eat; or how I had looked into the mirror at the point I thought I was ready to go, and suddenly felt I no longer had to.

"You mean like Abraham no longer having to kill his son?" I asked.

Francis nodded. "Something like that."

So he really did understand my case! I felt an outflowing of warmth for my friend, standing there with me on the bluff overlooking the sun glazed Pacific. "You don't realize what you've just done for me," I said, and bestowed on him a grateful hug.

My former classmate reciprocated, then resumed in the same low key, instructive tone: "Unless your submission is genuine, you won't get that release. Whoever or whatever is involved isn't easy to fool."

"That's what I'm afraid of," I sighed. "My release lasted only about twenty minutes before that irrational urge returned."

"I suppose you want to know if it was genuine," Francis said and shrugged. "I'm afraid nobody is in a position to tell."

"I guess not until it's too late to redeem yourself," I said, with put-on joviality. "Anyway, thanks for giving it to me straight, doctor."

My lighthearted appellation triggered an unexpected response. "In case you've wondered," Francis casually rejoined, "I don't practice conventional medicine anymore. Only enough to keep my hospital privileges. I used to be very good at cutting up my patients and giving them a bag for this, a bag for that, an artificial what have you. I had patients coming to me from all over the country, even some from abroad. I was saving my patients' lives, but I wasn't improving their lives. Now, I'm more interested in teaching them how to make the most of the time they have left. My practice consists more and more of just talking to patients."

"You mean the way you're talking to me?"

Francis looked out at the brilliance of the ocean reflecting the after-noon rays, then turned to me and nodded.

"So I really am here more as a patient than a friend?"

"What's the difference? Friend, patient, doctor. Doctor, patient, friend. That's what you are. That's what I am." He paused, then laughed. "This time around, let's just say you're here as a friend."

We resumed our walk, in silence for a while. We had to concentrate on our footing as we scampered single file down a steep, uneven path from the top of the bluff to the ocean's edge. But once we started on the hard, wet sand along the beach, Francis launched into a saga of his own. Yes, he also had been through an experience of this sort. As a doctor with scientific training, he had been especially skeptical about what was going on. Yet he could clearly recognize being temporarily endowed with precognition powers, such as the ability to tell who was behind a door or know when a phone was about to ring. Most astounding were episodes when he started burning up, with whiffs of heat coming out of his shoes and curling out from beneath the collar of his shirt. He would sometimes have to interrupt his consultation with a patient and run off to soak his feet.

God, I thought to myself, no wonder he understands my case! This guy is further gone than I. While I might have merely tried to humor him a few years back, I was listening to his every word as if what he had experienced held the key to my life.

"At one stage," Francis explained, as we neared the frontage of the LaJolla Beach and Tennis Club, "when things got heavy and I felt I was losing touch, I tried to turn it into a joke. I said, 'Hey God, I'm having a vision, aren't I?' You should have heard God bark me back in line. You're right, just like the old headmaster when he was mad at some poor lower-mid! For a while, I also thought I was Saint Francis. This puzzled me because my parents were Jewish. My St. Francis delusion certainly didn't come about from having been named after a spinster aunt from Italy."

I laughed. "I thought I was Saint Augustine. Yet he's the one I always blamed for trying to screw up the world with his anti-sex legacy." I stepped around a patch of foam deposited by the surf, then stopped. "We really sound like a couple of middle-aged nuts."

My former schoolmate also stopped. "I'll never be the same, if that's what you mean. Talking to patients about how to live and how to die is hardly as remunerative as cutting them up. I may have to sell the big house and pull back in other ways." Francis shook his head and smiled as if amused at himself. "When I was growing up, my old man owned a bar in Queens where his profits came from customers getting drunk. I really don't feel I can any more justify making a whole lot of money from my patients' maladies."

I couldn't resist. "Hey Buzzy," I exclaimed, "it seems we've ended up on parallel paths after all . . . and not too far apart!"

Now it was Francis who gave me a hug. Despite his assured exterior, I sensed Francis shared with me a certain fragility. His gesture gave added meaning to his words, *Doctor, patient, friend, what's the difference?*

We had passed the main complex of the LaJolla beach club and were standing in front of the panoramic window of the Marine Room. The sandy beach ended abruptly against a steep cliff, and we could go no further. How ironic! We were just a few feet from where the wife of my erstwhile sparring partner at Yale and I had renewed our relationship in the cocktail lounge on the other side of the huge window. That was more than twenty years ago, shortly after completing my three-year reserve stint in the Navy.

150

I could see the table where she and I sat, while she opined mournfully over margaritas that life was nothing but a dirty trick.

"I wouldn't want to change what I went through," Francis observed, as we turned to go back to his house. "I hope you'll eventually be grateful for what happened to you, too. Remember, we're merely reflecting a reality that others are afraid to recognize. Once we get enough people to acknowledge it exists, it will become the accepted reality, the new paradigm. What we need is a critical mass to get this transformation going in an irreversible way; the sooner the better."

5/

What I liked best about my Laguna Beach cottage was the feeling of openness and space. Across the entire front of this little house was a set of sliding glass doors that opened onto a spacious balcony about sixty feet above the Pacific. It was as if everything beyond that glass was an extension of where I lived, removing any barriers between me and the endless ocean and sky. From my balcony I could watch the way the surf would splinter against the rocks a few hundred yards beyond the beach, or survey the ever-changing texture of the distant horizon. And I never tired of observing the human activity on the crescent strip of sand below. This happened to be the same secluded beach I had considered such an ideal repository of potential brides just after leaving the Navy. They were still there, a new generation basking in the sun, their attributes intimately revealed by the latest in swimsuit wear. It was interesting to watch the subtle shift of who happened to be pairing up with whom on the towels for two. If only to keep the record straight, I myself paired up shortly after arriving from Coconut Grove. As in that misadventure with Sallie, it happened without premeditation and more or less by accident, and the subsequent feeling served as enough of a deterrent to have protected me since.

This was my second year in Laguna Beach, and that chastisement from beyond seemed increasingly remote. This was partly due to what I had recently heard described as the dynamics of becoming dulled, whereby an unacceptable reality is slowly pushed out of the mind. But my perspective was also changing. Perhaps I wasn't so unfortunate after all to have received that devastating call. Wasn't what I had experienced merely a preview of the ultimate call all of us would one day have to take? Wouldn't we all one day be similarly exposed, with no rug under which to sweep the debris of our imperfect lives? Maybe hell was nothing else than having to contemplate eternally how we had failed to measure up, eternally saddled with the sorrowful awareness of our sins. Yet I had been given a chance to amend my life and pursue a different path.

Though no longer fearful of any physical entanglement, I knew I still had to remain vigilant. From my few aberrant encounters, I had learned that a reluctant stance was the most seductive technique of all. This also gave me a polite excuse for keeping any relationship at the cheek kissing stage if the requisite inspiration wasn't there. Another benefit not to be overlooked was that I was gradually gaining the trust of husbands, too. Especially of white-haired Peter, the swinging developer entrepreneur across the street, who was married to an alluring woman half his age. On the discreet advice of a fat Indian guru who claimed wiry old Peter was dangerously toxic from his materialistic thoughts, his wife made him wear a prophylactic whenever they made love. During my first months as their neighbor, I was repeatedly surprised to find the sixty-year-old husband at my door, anxiously peering over my shoulder as he inquired if I hadn't seen his wife. Now, Peter frequently confided to me his version of their marital woes, while generously overlooking whatever implicit affection his wife's friendship for me entailed. Moreover, I was free to use the washing machine in his garage even when nobody was home.

Best of all, I was able to remain single-minded in my quest to share with others what I had so dramatically learned. My efforts on *Future Pleasure* about humanity's fulfilling destiny had morphed into a larger, partly pessimistic *Confessions of a Hapless Hedonist*. Drawing on my recent spiritual comeuppance, I was intent on showing how insignificant were the differences between people – between races, religions, nationalities, and whatever – when compared with the flawed tendencies we all shared. Whether or not labeled as the original sin that drove Adam and Eve to eat from the forbidden tree, it was this same human drive that built civilizations, but if left unchecked, could also lead to their demise. Despite its down-to-earth simplicity, the overarching concept I eventually formulated was beyond anything that I could have conjured up on my own. Here's partly what I wrote:

There is an unheralded, heretofore unnamed human affliction that has been causing havoc in our midst from earliest civilizations to this day. Designated by three words – Survival Overcompensation Trauma and its telling acronym SOT – this enduring condition may help explain why previous civilizations have failed and our own is not immune to this fate.

As the name implies, Survival Overcompensation Trauma is a disorder in which some of the basic responses originally developed to ensure our survival have gone awry. Activated by our desire to seek pleasure and avoid pain, these responses have become dangerously exaggerated and are far removed from the life-saving purpose they once had.

The emergence of SOT harks back to a deceptively logical assumption: that if one of something helped us to survive, twice as much — or more — should be correspondingly beneficial. No doubt, having more to eat and securing more favorable living conditions in an inhospitable world of pervasive scarcity and relentless toil has over the ages often spelled the difference between life and death. Yet in our bountiful world, the opportunity for large swaths of population to double or triple their calorie intake, while enjoying the luxury and comforts of a sedentary life, has contributed to increasing obesity, diabetes and other degenerative conditions. Despite countervailing trends toward healthful living, the legions of plump, comfort-seeking youth in thrall to their electronic devices are especially at risk to their own health as well as imperiling the country's future.

SOT has spread in our world to impact virtually every area of life. Thus if a Ford or a Toyota was essential for getting around, why not have a garage full of high-performance luxury cars? If a few hundred thousand dollars in the banking industry was considered an enviable salary, why not shoot for millions? If two nuclear bombs ended World War II, why not stockpile thousands? If one or two violent scenes helped a film succeed, why not feature violence throughout? No matter what the endeavor, whatever satisfied yesterday may no longer do so tomorrow, reinforcing the enduring desire for still more. Beyond producing an unfathomable array of social and emotional issues, these escalating demands are environmentally and financially unsustainable.

Yet the most consequential dimension of SOT derives from the fact that any pleasure compounded over time may have unforeseen moral consequences. The individual doses may seem harmless enough, but like radiation, the damage can accumulate and produce a single-mindedness that brooks no interference in the pursuit of self-seeking goals. That is the ultimate synergy of SOT. In this progressively deteriorating moral condition, otherwise upstanding individuals are liable to relinquish all sense of self-restraint and are ready to lie, to cheat, to steal, sometimes even to kill, in order to get whatever they crave. Their unprincipled quest for comforts and wealth is liable to be further compounded by the quest for power, whose ultimate synergy is reflected in that well-known adage, "Power tends to corrupt and absolute power corrupts absolutely. The combined effects of such heedless pursuit of SOT's self-serving goals by some of our most influential citizens are ubiquitous, compromising our public and private institutions while undermining the trust that is essential for our society to function.

Despite progress against the physiological excesses of SOT, thanks to the increasing emphasis on healthful living and conservation, there is no correspondingly accessible antidote against the moral dimension of SOT's ultimate synergy. Philosophers, theologians, and scholars of various stripes have continued to seek effective ways for treating this human affliction, in whatever guise it appeared, throughout history. It is perhaps telling that the world's three great monotheistic religions share the story of Adam and Eve's transgression in the Garden of Eden. Whether divinely inspired or set down by some astute observer as a rationale for the human condition, this somewhat muddled narrative may also be read as a metaphor for the original case of SOT. Though leading bountiful lives, that unwitting first couple was from the beginning susceptible to contagion with the desire for "more." In the Torah version, as well as in the expropriated Old Testament tale, they have been enjoined by God, on the pain

155

of death, not to eat or even touch the fruit from the tree in the middle of the garden. But lulled by the snake's wiles, Eve is impressed by how beautiful the tree looks, imagines how good its fruit would taste, and contemplates how wonderful it would be to become wise. In the Koranic adaptation, because of Satan's boast that he "will create in them false desires," Adam and his more suggestible companion have been warned not to even approach that tree of knowledge. And their fall into disfavor comes not just from eating the fruit from the forbidden tree but from having aroused their creator's concern that "man" would soon be "stretching out his hand" to eat from the tree of eternal life. Significantly, Adam and Eve's banishment from a life of plenty in both the Old Testament and Torah versions is into a harsh world of pain, scarcity, and lifelong toil. While Eve's heedless initiative presumably spared humanity from a static, witless existence – and was symbolic of one of the prerequisites for the rise of civilizations – today's compounding of those unbridled desires is threatening to bring about the demise of our own civilization, and again plunk us into a world of scarcity and toil. Thousands of years hence, should anyone care for a brief explanation for that inevitable demise, the Biblical tale of the Fall should say perfectly well just about all that needed to be said. Yes, they too had everything and wanted more.

While I didn't fantasize that this SOT theory could have ever made the optional reading list in Professor Baumer's class, it certainly seemed to be a useful shorthand for explaining what was happening in our world today.

6/

I hadn't forgotten my commitment to good works. I would be reminded of this long-ago pledge on seeing a busload of inner-city children disgorged on our crescent beach. Shouldn't I be one of those harried counselors watching over these exuberant eight-year-olds? As it was, I settled for trying to pacify some of the beach-going regulars over this noisy invasion of their turf.

My volunteer efforts with terminal indigents in Miami had come to a logical close with the death of Nikos, the former short order cook, followed by the negotiated end of my Coconut Grove lease. While I no longer felt the internal press to resume that aspect of my commitment, I tried to incorporate the spirit of the Florida endeavors into my daily life. This took no willful effort on my part, and more often than not, turned out to be fun. Like the time I loaned Susanne, a German war bride divorcee struggling to bring up her two boys, a thousand dollars to cover a cash and carry grocery bill at her quaint, sidewalk restaurant. Susanne was unfortunately becoming more interested in learning how to read past lives than in planning a menu for Sunday brunch, and eventually lost the place.

Then there was my friend Kenny, who felt uniquely connected to the image in the Shroud of Turin, which supposedly covered the body of the crucified Christ. Known as the Skipper, Kenny performed his unique hop in tattered sneakers and frayed designer shorts on the boardwalk of the town's Main Beach, imploring the throngs of beachgoers to help him build a better world. "Earth, earth, hear the word of truth! Only the truth will set you free!" he would begin, pumping his arm in sync with his fast-paced skipping, each stomp rhythmically jarring his beard and undulating his shoulder length hair like cresting waves of shimmering spray. "I know . . . I know . . . I know it's up to man to make his move and create a new heaven and a new earth. There will be a new vibration and we won't have all that destruction. It's up to us. It's up to us. Don't delay . . . don't hesitate," Kenny implored, having put his own spin on the Biblical prophecy that God would come to create a new heaven and a new earth. Kenny's compulsive gait and intense gaze made me think his skipping was no more voluntary than the holy gyrations of medieval victims of Saint Vitus's dance. "I need your vote!" he sounded off, as if addressing the world. "I'm running for the office of life consciousness . . . my only opponent is death."

There he was again, an overwrought Jesus look-alike hopping along the boardwalk at almost a run, shouting his message at beach-goers dozing off in the afternoon sun. "I'm free, I'm free, praise the Lord I'm free, this crazy mixed-up world ain't got no hold on me!" How indifferent this high school dropout and Vietnam ex-GI seemed to be to the materialistic world while preaching his truth! Skipping without a shirt even on the chilliest winter days, he appeared unconcerned about the food he picked out of trashcans, or the depressing shoebox-sized room in which he lived. He had spent most of the previous eight years on a steep, thousand-foot peak of rocks and scrub bushes behind the town's gentler residential hills. He was the only one to have evaded the police and fire department raids that cleared out the hippie commune occupying the hill in the late sixties and early seventies.

"Anybody who's ever come up here with me has been chosen by the Spirit," Kenny ceremoniously announced, as we finished our ascent and waded the final several yards through thick shrubs to a small clump of bushes. "That's where I used to sleep. I used to kind of fold everything up so they wouldn't see me. I had this old sleeping bag, and I really loved it under the stars.

Every morning when I woke up, I'd see this beautiful hummingbird hovering over my head. I know it was the same one, not just
because of the way he looked . . . or she, or whatever . . . but
because I felt like I got to know him . . . know him like a fellow
being . . . like I know you. And there he'd be, hovering over me,
sort of greeting me and letting me know the universe didn't forget
me. I called him my God bird. He would always hover and flutter
his wings, but one day he landed on the ground, only inches from
my face where I lay in my sleeping bag. He stopped fluttering his
wings and just looked at me to let me know he loved me and
trusted me. Then this God hummingbird began to dip his head
from side to side, from one side to the other . . . from one side to
the other . . . and every time he'd dip his head, he would take me
to a higher and higher awareness . . . Left, right . . . left, right . .
. left, right . . . left, right . . . I couldn't count the numbers of
dimensions where this bird was taking me. I was in another
world, and every time he'd dip his head, he'd take me to a still
different realm not attached to this world . . . a realm of harmony
and connection of all life. I was aware of everything that was in
the past, of everything in the present, of everything in the future.
It lasted no more than a few seconds, but it seemed like eternity."

Kenny paused and shook his head, as if trying to snap out of
a trance. "So the highest plane I ever experienced wasn't through
drugs or alcohol, not through readin' the Bible, not through
praying . . . but through this hummingbird. I had read the Word,
but this bird was the Word. The Bible says all creatures shall
bear witness to the creative force. Well, we were both bearing
witness to each other. And the hummingbird was saying, 'I leave
you now.' I knew he was going to leave that day and never return. But he left me with an illumination, with a new understanding of life and that we were surely one."

Within days of showing me his former hilltop retreat, the Skipper stopped skipping and began to wilt, as if drained of some energizing force within. At first I attributed his condition to the apparent lack of public response; yet his transformation was more profound. It was as if the Skipper had come to an abrupt awakening in an alien world and found himself saddled with the concerns of a materialistic life. He started to worry about his diet and increasingly resented the hovel in which he discovered himself to be living. His sleek, trained body began to stink, and no matter what measures he took, it continued to degenerate into a sickly mess. I drove him fifteen miles for free therapy to a chiropractor he had once met, and then offered to help him get to Georgia, where his widowed mother lived on Social Security.

"That's the power of the Spirit for you," Kenny sighed, as I waited with him at the boarding gate of the Los Angeles airport for his flight to Atlanta, while fellow passengers cast nervous glances at this haunting Jesus look-alike who would be on their plane. "No, I didn't stop skipping because I got discouraged, and I didn't get sick because I stopped skipping. The Spirit left me first. I felt it in my bones, in every ounce of me. The Spirit left me first! Only then did I get discouraged. And only after that did I get sick. Man, without that *durn* Spirit that comes down to you from out in the cosmos, you ain't nothing."

In trying to fathom the essence of Kenny's life, I could discern the shortcomings in mine; imperfections that were difficult to overcome and pleasures I was unwilling to forego – whether compensating on my own for my celibate state or pampering my palate. The temptation to gustatory excess was in fact greater since I had learned from Dr. Bieler about the principle of alkali reserve, which almost entirely removed any threat of gastric

160

distress. (Aside from the zucchini breakfast I had long since given up, this meant supplementing lunches and dinners with large quantities of watery vegetables, especially lettuce, green beans, celery and cucumbers.) At times I still overindulged in too much wine or took one too many drags on a powerful joint at white-haired Peter's. This led to uncontrollable appetite, which once compelled me to devour everything I could find in my neighbor Peter's house – including a whole jar of homemade fig jam he had been saving for some special occasion. I also succumbed to inexcusable pride, when I strongly hinted to Peter that what had kept his young wife on their side of the street was my self-restraint rather than his money, which as a successful industrialist he openly claimed. Of course, the following day I profusely apologized to my host, even though he had greeted me with a warm hug and repeatedly assured me I had nothing to apologize for.

7/

During my years in Laguna Beach, I had yet to miss Sunday mass; more accurately, Saturday evening mass, which had been officially approved in Rome as a substitute, leaving my Sundays free. Combined with the time in Miami, this devotional commitment was already lasting about as long as I had lugged around the pressure cooker for Dr. Bieler's zucchini diet. I was no less eager to recover from what I felt was still ailing me now. I even went to communion regularly, hoping it might speed up the process, though I still didn't know exactly what the process was that needed speeding up.

What brought about the astounding event I am about to relate would be difficult to say. It could have come from my twice-weekly sessions with Michael Wu Quinto, a Los Angeles acupuncturist I had befriended, who offered a special toning treatment for augmenting the potential of my brain. With the needles positioned just right in both ears, the procedure could leave a person feeling euphorically smart. At least that's how it sometimes worked for me – though this event that would affect me so lastingly could just as easily have been caused by the kind of life I had been trying to lead. Over the previous two weeks, I had deliberately refrained from any manual release of sexual tension while I concentrated on transcribing as faithfully as I could what I had learned firsthand about the role of pleasure in life. And only the evening before, during communion at Saturday mass, I received a message of sorts. Trying to remain unobtrusive in the crowded church, I was the last of more than a hundred people lining up to receive the holy host. Just as I reached the altar for my turn, the priest ran out of the consecrated wafers he had been dispensing from the gilded chalice in his hand. Now, I alone remained kneeling in front of the entire church as I waited for a fresh batch of the little round wafers to be transformed into the body of Christ. How embarrassed I would have been if some of my trendy friends from the beach wandered in just then! They might have mistaken me for another of those Christians unable to resist hinting at the superiority of their religion at the expense of other religions, denominations or sects. In that interminable minute or two on my knees, I also had a momentary shock. Perhaps this was God's way of telling me he didn't want me to engage in this charade anymore; that I was a phony at heart, unworthy of his gifts. But in the next instant I was filled with a lighthearted pride, a feeling that perhaps this was God's way of singling me out and letting me know I was on the right path.

The following day, I augmented this optimistic mood with an exceptionally powerful coffee fix. It was a Sunday mid-morning late in spring, a sunny day with persistent patches of fog hugging the coast. Resting in the warm sand at the secluded end of Main Beach, I shifted my gaze from the pelicans perched on the rocky ledge beyond the breaking surf to the hilly skyline of houses and shrubs looming over the town. Amid the silhouetted greenery, a window glittered here and there, bright, pinkish reflectors penetrating the obscuring mist. I was feeling detached, absorbing the sound of the ocean and the cool seaweed texture of the air, just as my friend Cliff broke his stride in his five-mile jog and paused to chat. "Hey man, the guys are hassling me again on account of their women giving me the eye," he complained. Cliff's six-foot-two body of gracefully muscled ebony tapered to a narrow waist had placed him in a predicament I could appreciate. "You don't seem too upset," I countered with a laugh, and then watched him saunter off toward the crowds.

As I stood up to start down the beach, I was feeling more and more as an observer in this human drama that I was still trying to comprehend. I was experiencing an overwhelming gratitude for finding myself in such a special place. No matter what the future might hold, I wanted to remember the magnificence of being here and have no regrets for having failed to realize that.

It was while strolling along this partly fogged in beach that I felt an enlightenment slowly but palpably permeating my consciousness. It was an inspiration I sensed descending from above, not unlike what had preceded my harrowing excoriation by God; something shifting directly overhead to create an opening in the sky. I had the vibrant feeling of being in the path of a radiant beam focused directly on my brain. And this time the news was good, heralding a transforming event akin to what I had experienced at my sister's Cape Cod prayer group. Imbued with a sudden exhilaration for the sanctified name I had struggled only the previous day to mutter in church, I was filled with a fathomless serenity, surrounded by an aura that made me immune to the concerns of this world. It was a sensuous emotion, yet not desirous of any physical satisfaction as such. The feeling itself offered satisfaction enough, crowding out all competing desires and thoughts. I was suffused with an overwhelming gratitude, a blithesome lightheadedness, knowing that no travail would be too onerous to bear. How well I understood what those joyful charismatics in Miami, especially my friend Sol, had meant about Jesus walking at their side! There wasn't anything I could possibly ask for or want. My sole desire was to share this feeling with others, to reveal to them this astounding good news. I felt capable of extraordinary communication, free of any barriers or bounds, full of joyful understanding even for people I might have otherwise considered crass. And the news I had to share was good indeed, regardless of the precise identity of Jesus Christ. It made little difference whether Jesus, known as Yeshua in his day, was the Son of God, or a part alien endowed with some supergene from outer space, or whether he was an all too human rabbi inspired in a unique way. It seemed immaterial whether Jesus had continued to exist in our midst as an illuminating spirit from above, or his verbal legacy had the power to activate this joyfully pervasive emotion within my brain. Those were the kinds of details beyond the grasp of the human mind over which people had tortured and killed each other in the past. What I could exultantly vouch for was that this Jesus-emotion suffusing my brain had the power to mediate on our behalf with the stern and uncompromising God I had experienced on that snowy Massachusetts field, whether that happened to be the inexorable Yahweh of Hebrew Scriptures and the Old Testament, or still another emotive force within my brain. This Jesus-emotion was an antidote to primitive human wrath bent on enforcing God's will, whether embodied in an Inquisition torturer or a militant jihadist incited by some Ayatollah's fundamentalist paean. This Jesus emotion was a gloriously saving grace, a force of which we could avail ourselves to find forgiveness for our most troubling frailties and sins. It was a vibrant, liberating feeling through and through.

As I continued down the crowded beach in my exuberant mood, I felt an inkling of a privileged truth. Perhaps earth really was a training ground for a higher universal role, a place where incarnated souls – those individual packages of evolving human consciousness – had to learn to correct basic flaws inherent in their design. I was beginning to understand how God, whether a personified supreme being or a non-corporeal force, or some superhuman intelligence from an unimaginably advanced civilization on a planet spinning around an unknown star, might have sent a special signal, an emissary, even a speck of his own essence to become incorporated in a human son, who would show us how to overcome that array of flaws to which he also was heir.

Trekking along the ocean's edge with this scenario in mind, I wondered, how could I have been ashamed to utter Christ's name? He was the trendiest of all – and so much more! Jesus's messianic mission had been not only to free us from our original sin, but to reorient us in a way that would lead us to a higher, incomparably more satisfying goal. Yes, we had to be reborn from above to overcome the elemental pleasures of our primitive origins, those compulsive demands of our Survival Overcompensation Trauma – of our enduring SOT – in order to move to the next stage of humanity's aspirations and fulfill our unforgoable place in the heavens among its stars and galaxies. Perhaps God

awaited us there, and awaited us impatiently to fulfill our ultimate role of helping him run the universe.

Striding on the damp, firm sand just beyond the ocean's edge,
I felt a breathtaking buoyancy for having grasped the potential
of our fate. Still enthralled through and through by that joyous
bond with Jesus-the-Christ, I felt myself straighten up, so the
hordes of Sunday beachgoers wouldn't think me a slouch. Now if
only those legions of worshippers, who so religiously repeated
that sanctified name would no less faithfully follow in their redeemer's steps, embracing devotees embarked on other paths in
that same radiantly fulfilling spirit that would render irrelevant
any claims who might be right or wrong, even more or less – the
reorientation process could at last begin without anyone having
missed a turn.

Within six months of that enlightening day, I was no longer going to church. Yes, the Church had been a welcome place for me
to seek refuge in a storm, and I wasn't sure that if another per-
turbation in my life threatened before I died, I wouldn't again
try to seek refuge in this childhood bastion of certitude. But right
now I sensed an unbridgeable disconnect. The Jesus I had experienced was a joyous one of universal love, laying down no doctrinaire prerequisites and holding forth an all-encompassing embrace [some thirty years before Pope Francis!]. The Christ I had
encountered in the Church was the depressing, doctrinaire one on
the cross, so often used for man's purposes and misdeeds. I realized, of course, that the foregoing may have merely been a con-
venient rationale, an explanation used as an excuse for my un-
willingness to inconvenience myself. And if this indeed were the
case, I trusted that my ever-forgiving Jesus – whose unforgetta-
ble intercession continued to influence my daily life – would

understand and in his mercy intercede again before the fear of the unknown would reduce me to my knees.

8/

There was panic on my little crescent beach, a sudden scampering and yelling as men, women and children in unruly little groups tried to evade an unexpected wave. As I watched the bedlam while treading water just beyond the turbulence of the cresting waves, I wondered: Is this what the end was going to be like? The way those people screamed and scurried around as if about to be smothered by that ultimate wave – the towering wall of swirling green water that supposedly would one day engulf California and wrench it from the United States. Yet these beachgoers had merely been trying to keep from getting wet; to move their towels, picnic baskets, and tanning oils out of the path of a wave surging unexpectedly far. They were now back in their little groups, beyond the water's reach, enjoying the sun. That they were somehow being given a second chance surely didn't cross their minds.

I had now been in Laguna Beach almost four years, and my sojourn there was coming to an end. I was feeling sufficiently grounded in normal life, and it was time to start replenishing my nearly exhausted freedom buffer in the bank. Convincing potential clients to hire me would be more demanding now that I felt obliged to make it clear up front I wasn't prepared to exaggerate, twist, misstate, or otherwise compromise the truth for a client's cause. My most promising prospect was a low budget producer in Florida. Although the circumstances related to directing one of his videos would eventually lead to changing my life, I wasn't earning enough to start replenishing that nearly exhausted freedom buffer. When I received word that Mother broke her hip and I returned home to Massachusetts to help out during her convalescence, a confluence of events led to a drastic decision. With Mother imploring me to remain indefinitely – and the owner of my little abode in Laguna Beach threatening to convert it into a more lucrative weekly summer rental – the practical solution was to stay at home and pursue my freelance interests from there. But what finally nudged me to give up that idyllic life in Laguna Beach was discovering I had a knack for selling Father's exercise equipment.

Father was reaping benefits of his adopted country's exercise boom. In addition to Mr. Exercycle, he had become Mr. Trotter Treadmill and stocked his enlarged showroom with an array of physical fitness equipment from leading manufacturers in the field. He continued to demonstrate the Exercycle in people's homes and could still maneuver the weighty machine without help. His ploy of pulling out his driver's license with its 1897 birthdate was becoming more and more effective with each passing year. While making a demonstration to one youngish couple, the wife watched Father as the seat bucked him up and down like a bronco, the pedals went around and around, and his head flew forcefully back and forth with the movement of the handlebars. She grew increasingly concerned, and after a few moments called out to her husband, "Honey, honey, please, quick, buy the machine before the old gentleman kills himself!"

Father was feeling financially secure. The mortgage on the farm had been recently paid off, and yes, the mahogany chest with the massive family silver for twenty-four had been retrieved from the pawnbroker in the nick of time eons ago and remained unopened in a closet since then. Father was now back to his generous ways (if not exactly as the patron of the arts he once had been in Prague) bestowing Christmas checks on shipping clerks and secretaries at the Exercycle and Trotter headquarters, and bottles of vintage French champagne on the respective presidents. For the svelte African-American woman who dealt with Father on behalf of the Boston Globe in placing his weekly ads, it was a bottle of Shalimar perfume.

Considering all that Father had come through in such a singular way, I couldn't avoid the conclusion that luck, providence, or whatever controlled human fate must have been on his side. The most convincing evidence of this unseen hand appeared whenever I accompanied him on the drive to Boston. In pulling out of our obscured driveway, Father was already at risk. Rather than carefully inching out and trying to glimpse right and left through the surrounding bushes, he leaned on his horn for a prolonged toot. "That's their business to watch out," he explained, if I happened to shake my head. On the thruway to Boston, Father abruptly switched lanes without looking, and depending on his mood, slowed down or speeded up. On the less traveled stretches, he devoted an alarming amount of attention to *The New York Times*, propped up on the steering wheel. My only rational explanation why we made it to our destination was that any driver near our erratically moving car must have decided to stay clear. Still, how could that account for the fact that in his forty years in the exercise business, during which he averaged more than 50,000 miles each year, Father had managed to come through with only dents and scrapes to his car?

Father enjoyed an unshakable peace of mind. "Can you imagine what would have happened if instead of Mother I had married some painted-up woman who wanted to go to parties?" I heard him periodically wonder out loud. "But I already knew that when I first spotted her getting on the tram." Whenever I

169

now inquired how he slept, Father smugly replied, "Don't ask stupid questions," — meaning, that except for getting up once to relieve his aging prostate, he didn't wake up between going to bed around midnight and rising usually before dawn. Yet the most significant change from the way Father had felt during his desperate beginnings in the United States would have remained unnoticed if I hadn't pointed it out: No longer did he crinkle his cheeks into that nervous grimace that turned his eyes into slits.

"I never dreamed I would have such a fulfilling old age," Father reiterated with genuine wonder.

As soon as Mother no longer needed my daily care, I returned to Laguna Beach to pack up my things. In giving up my ocean-side perch and saying final good-byes, I reflected once more on life in this exotic, festive place. Even the personalized license plates on the BMWs and other cars wending their way along Pacific Coast Highway seemed to have a certain flair, whether CRE8INK, ENLITND, or ATTITUD. Not surprisingly, there also was B42LATE. And what an ideal time to be alive! For only a dollar thirty-five, I could buy a loaf of still-warm-from-the-oven Dutch whole wheat bread at Stadelman's bakery on South Coast Highway, a few blocks from where I lived. This bread was as good as any in the world, especially if it didn't completely rise and wouldn't be quite so full of air. Ironically, that's when it was on sale at one third off. And for four dollars, I could have a five-gallon jug of water, fresh from a mountain spring, delivered to my door. And a quarter-a-day would plop hundred pages of *Los Angeles Times* into my driveway at dawn.

How easy it was to have these things, how hard not to take them for granted! And I wondered, what would that newspaper, the water, and the bread be worth tomorrow if we were to sustain some catastrophe before the end of the day?

I recalled with a sense of nostalgia the era of a few decades ago, when THE END IS NEAR was touted almost exclusively by a few scraggly characters, holding up crudely lettered placards or parading their message on sandwich boards. They preferred to position themselves in places where they could best confront the people most addicted to the luxuries of modern life, be it on Fifth Avenue in New York in front of the sparkling displays of Tiffany's and Cartier's, or near the George V Hotel in Paris, where the message was *La Fin S'Approche*. They tried to catch your eye with their flimsy signs and perhaps rivet you with a fleeting glance, hoping it would remain stored deep within your mind, and from time to time, pop disturbingly into your consciousness. No wonder most passersby wanted to avoid these scruffy sign-toters, perhaps crossing the street or inwardly laughing them off.

The possibility of the human experience winding down was no longer a crackpot thought. All anyone had to do was to pick up the morning newspaper. President Reagan was finishing his first term, and the vast military buildup to confront the Evil Empire was in full swing. A MIG fighter plane had shot down a Korean airliner with U.S. citizens aboard, and Soviet troops were locked in hot combat with our surrogates in Afghanistan. The arsenals of each side were stocked with more than ten thousand nuclear weapons targeted at each other's cities and sensitive sites. From my days as a young naval officer on a refueling ship stationed at Bikini during the next-to-last series of open-air nuclear tests, I could graphically recall what just one of those so-called devices could do! Would the end come as abruptly as that unexpected wave I had witnessed on the beach, or more poignantly, as John F. Kennedy's death — cheering and carefree smiles

171

transformed in an eye-blink into incredulous, agonized gasps? Or would it be more gradual, perhaps a global economic collapse caused by the spending and borrowing frenzy that ignored the basic premise that if you take out a loan and incur a debt, you have to pay it back? The end could also come from some ecological disaster from having unwisely tampered with nature too long to satisfy our unbridled desires and needs.

Was there truly no alternative? Was our unforgoable role among the stars to remain unfulfilled? Would the hope of my friend Kenny the Skipper, the high school dropout, for man to make his move and create a new heaven and a new earth remain unrealized? Was it too late for a transforming new reality, a new paradigm to be adopted, as yearned for by my former boarding school classmate, the LaJolla surgeon Francis G? Was a human caused Armageddon as inevitable as had been predicted since earliest times? Were we powerless victims and culprits both, destined to succumb to our flaws? To rephrase the question: Were we doomed always to live in a world where we suffered and died because there wasn't enough — or in a world where we suffered and died because we didn't know how to handle plenitude? Were we forever caught between the scourge of scarcity on the one hand, and on the other, the debilitating excesses to which we were driven by our Survival Overcompensation Trauma — by our enduring SOT? Were we forever doomed to share the fate of Sisyphus working his rocky burden to the mountain's peak, only to have it come crashing back?

PART THREE
1989 - 1996

1/

My first trip back to Prague following the Velvet Revolution was with Mother's ashes that were to be given a permanent place of repose in the family tomb. How ironic that Mother had been the only one in the family who believed that we would ever return! Before she fell and broke her second hip that led to her death, I had occasionally suggested she make the trip back to the one place where she might feel comfortable again. But her answer was always the same. "Do you think I'm going to let people see me as an old wreck?" Mother also had a secret fear that on deplaning at the airport in Prague, some Czech official would say to her, "How do you do?" and she would freeze and forget her English. Mother's trauma dated back to when she had first taken up with Father and he bemoaned her lack of languages that would hold him back in his political ambitions in Prague. Intensely proud, Mother sought to remedy the situation throughout her years on the farm by finding time to study languages on her own, and ended up subscribing to magazines from Spain, France, Germany, and the USSR.

The beginning of the end for Mother came when she again fractured her hip. Unlike the successful first operation, this one left her legs paralyzed, while the medication she was given for pain disoriented her mind. She wailed about an old geezer with a wicker basket on his back tracking her down, and begged me not to let him throw her into some cold, dank cellar. But then on one visit to the hospital, Mother greeted me with a strange alertness. "Come on, you're late!" she said with obvious impatience. "Don't you know the show must continue? Quickly, we must go back on stage."

"On stage?"

"You fool! How do you think anyone could make it through life if it wasn't only a play?"

In disposing of Mother's belongings as executor of her estate, I was struck by the methodical order in which she had kept her things. The tidy closets and neat chests of drawers in her room made me realize what agony Father's mess must have been for her through life. Mother assumed that anyone walking past our house and glancing in through the windows would attribute the disorder to the way she had been brought up – and commiserate with the count. That's why she had always tried to keep the shades drawn on the lower floor.

But it was in Mother's sewing materials – amid impeccably ordered boxes of buttons, needles carefully stuck in pin cushions, neatly rolled up pieces of leftover cloth, and other such paraphernalia – that I found a compactly wrapped bundle that touched me the most. It consisted of dozens of usable collars she had removed from shirts we could no longer wear. This little bundle rolled back the time until I had Mother once again before my eyes mending our clothes, scrimping every penny she could, and never buying anything for herself.

In reflecting on the course of Mother's life and how she had rebuffed the Count's entreaties for almost five years before becoming the mother of his children, I wondered: would she have ever accepted that role had she known what it would entail?

2/

Within a month of Mother's death, Father had sold his exercise business and was leaving Massachusetts to return permanently to Prague. In the three years since the Velvet Revolution brought down the Communist regime, he had gone back several times to file for restitution of his properties. Each time, he was greeted with a mixture of incredulity and awe, as if he were a modern day Odysseus returning home. One of those visits had been courtesy of the Czech government, when President Václav Havel bestowed on him the nation's highest honor, the Order of T. G. Masaryk. At that ceremony, Father was seated next to another esteemed recipient, Alexander Dubček, who led the country in 1968 into the liberalization of the Prague Spring. On being introduced to this heroic figure, whose attempts to give Communism a human face were crushed by invading Soviet troops, Father poked him in the stomach and said, "Ach, you really screwed it up! I could have been home twenty years sooner."

Father wasn't returning merely to expire in the country of his birth. When I drove him to the Boston airport, this ninety-five-year-old talked incessantly about refurbishing his properties and helping his native country regain its self-confidence. As he was about to board his flight, Father turned to me and sighed, "Just think what I could do if I was only eighty five!"

More so than any other returning emigrant, this former Exercycle salesman from New England had soon become a national hero. He had captured the hearts of the populace by promptly handing over our Renaissance palace to the National Theater for the next twenty years at a symbolic rent of one crown per year. And he stipulated a similar arrangement for his ivy-covered castle in the former Sudetenland, so that it could continue to serve as a retirement home for the mentally afflicted. The generosity of these gestures appeared all the more pronounced in a country where the nobility had been vilified over the previous four decades as incorrigible exploiters, and where former émigrés now rushing back to Prague to make their claims were often depicted as gold diggers.

Father's age was also a great asset. The media never tired of quizzing him about his diet or photographing him doing his daily miles on the stationary bicycle he had brought with him from the United States. Indeed, Father was proud of his continued vigorous health. While he could still read a telephone directory without glasses, he compensated for his partial loss of hearing by telling everyone, including the country's president, that they mumbled. "I didn't understand a word you said," I heard Father interrupt Václav Havel on the video my brother Tom was shooting of their initial meeting. "Why don't you speak clearly the way I've heard you on television." When the nervous president takes out a pack of cigarettes, Father instantly groans, "Ach, Jesus Maria!" The former playwright-dissident looks exasperated and may well have been reminded of his years as a political prisoner. But Father presses on: "You know, in America intelligent people don't smoke anymore. My father smoked five packs-a-day and died of lung cancer at fifty-seven." When the president tries to defend himself by saying he'd recently had a physical and his lungs were found to be in order, Father dismisses his words with an abrupt wave of the arm. "When they do find something, it will be too late. We need you too much."

3/

Never one to mince his words, Father was apt to be even more personally forthright with me. "You really look good," he said, as he eyed me across the dinner table at our restituted villa toward the end of my first week in Prague. "I think you still have it in you to make a son or two." "In that case," I shot back, "the credit goes to Barbara for resurrecting my life."

"Oh Barbara, Barbara!" Father retorted.

"Listen, if she had asked you in for a cup of tea during her time at Wellesley when you were selling Exercycles, you would have taken it as a great personal success."

"Hah!" Father exclaimed scornfully. "Barbara would have never bought an Exercycle. She's a Yankee. She wouldn't want to spend the money."

"That's probably true," I admitted. "But look how she has improved my life."

"The point is, she's too old to have children."

This had been Father's increasingly insistent refrain about Barbara, who was close to my age, since I first met her during one of my forays from Laguna Beach to work with that low-budget producer in Florida, where I interviewed her for a political action video.

"Just because you sleep with her," Father continued, "doesn't mean you have to marry her. And even if you do, that's no reason why you can't make a son or two on the side."

"Sometimes I don't think you realize what you're saying."

Father was undeterred. "If you promised to make some heirs, I could sign over to you a piece of Dianaberg right away," Father said, referring to the thousands of hectares of forests and agricultural land in the former Sudetenland.

I shook my head and wordlessly stared back.

Beyond my stolid response, I wasn't angry at this not-so-subtle bribery attempt. I realized Father was merely being consistent with what he had always urged me to do, and he wasn't about to change at ninety-five. To have children, especially male heirs, was his lifelong ultimate aim, and fulfilling it justified whatever means had to be employed. Although family tradition would have favored my older brother, who was busy with his lawyering in the United States – while two of his three adult children were already starting their own careers in Prague – I knew Father was in the process of transferring his properties to my younger brother Tom, which he wanted to accomplish for tax purposes before he died. Tom had forsaken his Miami Beach oceanfront condo – along with his carefree, well-paid gigs as cameraman-director – and was helping Father in such tasks as cutting through the Kafkaesque bureaucratic maze to get permits for refurbishing our long-neglected office buildings, freeing tenants trapped there in a stalled, sixty-year-old elevator, or going to the French store to buy Father a piece of scrod, trucked in daily from Paris.

"I'm perfectly happy if Tom runs everything," I said as an after-thought." Mother always believed his day would come." Although Tom had often worked for me as a cameraman, ours had been a warm, brotherly relationship, and I would defer to him just as often as he would to me. Athletic, personable, and conversant in a half-dozen languages, (which he had picked up while roaming around Europe for three self-sustaining years instead of opting for college) he was the one with star-power in the family.

For a moment, Father looked glum. "I'm no longer so sure he's going to produce either."

Indeed, Father's sole reservation about Tom was that at fifty, he was still looking for the ideal bride, just as I had been for so many years before meeting Barbara. What redeemed Tom in Father's eyes was that he had already busied himself interviewing an array of candidates in Prague, all of whom appeared to be in the early part of their childbearing years.

Father's outlandish offer dangled before me periodically in various forms had been welcome in one respect: Having turned down the opportunity to acquire substantial wealth, no one could say that this former civilian of fortune (as dubbed years ago by one of my friends) had paired up with such an accomplished woman as Barbara for questionable goals. The decision hadn't been at all difficult, and I never had second thoughts. I was daily acknowledging my gratitude for this relationship that had been fulfilling my life for almost a decade. *Deo Dato*, or gift of God, was the only way I could explain this most improbable of unions (with apologies to St. Augustine). Beyond our mutual attraction in looking at each other, Barbara had been raised with the sort of values I had recently come to embrace, and we were looking in the same direction. And having also been the founder of a leading center for the study of women's issues, she was daily enhancing my awareness and understanding in other subtle ways. As for my younger brother, his life certainly hadn't improved in Prague as heir apparent to the family estate. Even in his favorite pursuit, he had a far richer variety of options in the carefree atmosphere of Miami Beach than under the watchful scrutiny of his life in Prague.

Despite Father's determination to behave correctly during Barbara's visits for my sake, his frustration at seeing his son involved in what he considered a sterile relationship showed through. "Why do you always have to mumble?" he would reproach Barbara at the start of virtually every conversation. And indeed, Barbara did speak in measured tones, having been accustomed in her various professional roles to have her listeners' attention. Raising her voice to compensate for Father's hearing loss was for her a strain, and I tried to minimize the conversations between Father and her in whatever way I could. A climax of sorts came at breakfast one morning when Father seemed to be particularly hard of hearing. He had just posed a question to Barbara about her work with a Florida commission on equal rights, and as usual, she paused to think over her answer while taking another sip of coffee. When I seized this opportunity to jump in with an answer in Barbara's stead, Father immediately cut me off. "Can't a big shot like Barbara speak for herself?"

"I'm afraid not," I said, shaking my head. Seeing Father's attention suddenly piqued, I paused before adding significantly, "You see, she mumbles."

And I solidified another conclusion: not only did sudden great wealth – especially when augmented by an enviable title – rarely improve the quality of one's life, it failed even more consistently to improve character. This was increasingly evident in the way Father was beginning to take for granted being deferred to obsequiously at every turn. While he had remained notably outspoken in the United States, the imperatives of having to earn a living had placed restraints on how far he might let some of his more peremptory instincts reign. I didn't blame Father now any more than I blamed my younger brother Tom, from whom I was beginning to feel estranged for his increasing obsession with acquiring all of the property. I should also admit that the proliferation in my direction of Mr. Count this and Mr. Count that during the three weeks I was there didn't leave me entirely unscathed, and I would at times catch myself also taking my prerogatives for granted.

4/

My frequent sojourns in Prague with Father and Tom were at least partly in connection with my literary endeavors. Already on my first trip with Mother's ashes, I had explored the possibility of taking advantage of our name recognition and publishing some of my autobiographical work. An editor with a reading knowledge of English eventually managed to convince a leading publisher to take on a compact manuscript I had extracted from the much longer *Confessions of a Hapless Hedonist,* with a title loosely translated as *Confessions of a Frivolous Nobleman.*

In those early years following the Velvet Revolution, translators still occupied an enviable niche. Over the previous four decades behind the Iron Curtain, they represented a vaunted window on the outside world. In promoting a Shakespearean play, the translator's name was liable to appear more prominently on the marquee than that of the director and leading man. My translator was an elderly lady whose intent was to follow the accepted practice of imposing her voice over the author's and making the book her own. She also took it on herself to try to improve my prose whenever she didn't consider it dignified enough for a count. With hardly anyone over the years in a position to question a translator's work, the most she had come to expect were a few stylistic adjustments from the supervising editor. But loyal to the admonition of my old headmaster, the Duke, to keep up my Czech, I was in a position to propose literally hundreds of changes. This was a brash affront, and I had to take full advantage of being Mr. Count in exploiting the patience of my beleaguered translator.

I nevertheless ended up being grateful – and not only for the resulting quality of my translator's work. Our give-and-take enabled me to improve my command of the language to the extent that I could answer questions in hour long radio interviews without seriously messing up. And while on the air, I never missed an opportunity to further utilize what I had learned from the Duke.

"Don't think that because you're going to be richer and more powerful or perhaps have more education than most people," I often cited him during interviews as telling his privileged boys, "you will also somehow be better than they. The only way you can do that is by being less selfish and more humble than they." In a country recently under the impression that a TV episode of Dallas reflected the sum total of the United States, the Duke's words came as quite a surprise.

With my book soon topping the best-seller list, Father didn't disguise his pride and again renewed his offer of a substantial portion of the properties.

"I'm sorry you can't accept things the way they are," I replied on one such occasion. "You're depriving yourself of a chance to get to know a person I think you'd really like."

"You could still have a wonderful life ahead of you here," Father forged ahead. "You wouldn't have to worry about money, you're now famous in your own right, and everyone loves to see you in Prague whenever you come." Father gave me a significant look. "I think you could have any woman here you want!"

I realized Father was trying to pay me a compliment. "I'm doing just fine, thanks," I said, and left it at that.

The series of improbable coincidences I am about to relate occurred on my next trip to Prague; this time, to launch the publication of my second extracted-and-cobbled-together book, *Confessions of a Czech American*, and also to deliver in manuscript form the final part of what was becoming a trilogy.

I had an appointment to meet in the National Library with a seasoned observer of the Czech literary scene, Milena Nyklová. Several days earlier, she had interviewed me about the forthcoming book and related themes, just as she had done after the

publication of the first confessional volume. Now, having negotiated my way through the vast baroque library complex, I had
in my hands Milena Nyklová typed version of our conversation
for authorization.

I was particularly grateful for this opportunity to look over
what I had said, which was standard practice harking back to
the Communist regime. My intent wasn't to strike out anything
stupid or politically embarrassing but to ensure I had expressed
myself in Czech approximately the way I would if the interview
had been conducted in English. While my command of the language had continued to improve, I relied on my interviewers for
the occasional mot juste or the unstilting of a phrase.

Milena Nyklová seemed to have done a remarkable job. As I
sat next to this erudite, grandmotherly woman at one of the long
tables perusing her single-spaced pages in the quiet of the library's main reading room, only once did I feel constrained to
lean toward her and point to a sentence. That's where she had me
citing the seventeenth century philosopher, Jan Amos Komenský, about something called *eyeglasses of general deception*.

"I've never cited Komenský in my life," I whispered.

She smiled and nodded. "But the idea you express here is exactly the same as his."

I felt no urgency to press the issue in the hushed nave-like
room. But later that day, as I went about my errands in the city,
I felt increasingly uneasy about the Komenský quote. After all,
I had neither the inclination nor the academic wherewithal to
cite Komenský. In Baumer's intellectual history class, Komenský – or Comenius, as he was known outside his country – rated
no more than part of one lecture, and on the few occasions I had
noted his name in my various readings in subsequent years, it

185

was only because of his Czech origin rather than any kinship for his ideas.

When I returned home to our restituted wooden villa, I phoned Milena Nyklová. "As much as I appreciate the honor," I explained, determined to make my position clear about the Komenský quote, "I don't want to appear smarter than I am."

"But it's such a trifle," she rejoined. "It's perfectly normal to make far greater enhancements."

"Believe me, I'm grateful for any enhancement, as long as it's consistent with my capabilities. But quoting Komenský is not one of them. Whether regrettably or otherwise, I know almost nothing about him."

"Even so, I was astonished how often you sounded like him." She paused. "But that's all right. I'll put it in an editorial note instead."

Later that same week at my *autogramiada* at one of the largest bookstores in Prague, I was being assisted by Míla Tuzarová, a diminutive, energetic woman with short bleached hair, who had played a similar role at the signing of my first book. Standing alongside my table amid the floor-to-ceiling stacks, she handed me each of the books and helped me spell some of the trickier Czech names, as for example, *Paní Sylvii, Milé Jitce*. She kept the line moving and enabled me to devote myself momentarily to each recipient of a book.

Because of Míla's size, her head remained close to mine as we bantered back and forth, reflecting an evident concordance between us. That seemed to encourage some of the shyer readers to speak up while having their copy of the book inscribed.

The signing had started at 3:30, a half hour ahead of time, and continued for another half hour past the store's six o'clock closing. As Míla and I relaxed and sipped champagne brought by one of the patrons, she suddenly reached down to a nearby lower shelf and retrieved a glossy black volume. "I think this will interest you," she said, placing the heavy book on the table in front of me. "It's a wonderfully lively study of the work of Jan Amos Komenský. It was published in nineteen-eighty-seven . . . one of those remarkable books that every now and then made it through some crack past the officialdom."

"It must have caused a sensation," I ventured.

Míla pursed her lips and gave me a level stare. "Remember, that was two years before our Velvet Revolution. People usually ignored books published officially. The underground presses, the samizdat, that's where the action was. The publisher in this case printed twenty-five thousand, and five years later, most of them were still unsold. They were going to be shredded, but my boss loves books, and he managed to save several hundred."

I glanced at the main title, *Pictorial Atonement*. The smaller print explained it was a book of photographs on the theme of one of Komenský's works, *General Consultation about the Improvement of Human Affairs*.

My interest was piqued. It was only days ago that Milena Niklová had alerted me to my intellectual kinship with Komenský. Shouldn't I at least try to find out a bit more about this obviously wise, seventeenth-century itinerant Czech?

I opened the heavy cloth binding and started to turn the glossy pages of the oversized book. Interspersed with the promised photographs was one quote my eye immediately seized on: "If we are destined to wise up eventually, why not wise up now?" My God, that could have been uttered by my old headmaster, the Duke!

"Would you like to have the book?" Míla asked.

"I think I've just enough money for the taxi home."

"For you, Mr. Count, it's a gift." Then she quickly added, "A small token for helping us sell so many books."

What had prompted Míla Tuzarová to pick out this particular book from the thousands within easy reach in that part of the store? The uncanny coincidence of the two encounters with Komensky's works reminded me of the way I had picked out at random Thomas Merton's monastic autobiography, The *Seven Storey Mountain,* from Father's living room mess. To be sure, I had been in a spiritual turmoil then, foundering and desperately seeking help – whereas now I was at peace in the comfort of our restituted villa on the outskirts of Prague, reinforced by a Becherovka-and-orange juice mix, an original adaptation of this world-famous Czech liqueur. The kinship I was now feeling for so many of Komensky's assessments and ideals made me readily understand what had prompted Mrs. Nyklová to meld his words with mine. How glad I was I hadn't known of Komenský's works before now. In the country of his birth, where his precepts were so widely known, I might have been charged not only with ex-propriating his ideas in my two books, but with plagiarizing his very words. The manuscript of my prospective third volume that I had brought to Prague to be translated was rife with no less striking similarities, starting with the title, *Confessions of an Un-witting Sinner.* "What abundance there is of those who love the darkness of being unwitting," observed Komenský in Míla's gifted tome. "The world is full of altogether unwitting asses . . . Unless we can overcome being so unwitting, we will destroy our-selves." Komenský's diagnosis of our human condition also sounded familiar: "People for the most part are not mindful of their higher nature and have such an enslaved spirit that they succumb to the most worthless things, such as the stomach, over-indulgence and other trifles, by which they allow themselves to be ruled, led, pushed and pulled this way and that way." His conclusion about the futility of humanity's struggles was not un-like what I had concluded in my most depressed state, when I felt to be in league with Buddha: "What are the usual human endeavors that rule the world? Pursuit of property, valuables and delights. They pursue shadows instead of substance, and in their dedication to such worthlessness, they themselves dissolve into nothing."

Echoes of SOT, of our enduring malady, Our Survival Over-compensations Trauma? More than ever, Komenský seemed to be speaking to our world in our time.

Mrs. Tuzarová's gift inspired me to search out Komenský's other books after returning to the United States, with the intent of appending his thoughts in a postscript to my third volume. The two works I managed to track down (under the Comenius version of the author's name) were *The Great Didactic* and *Labyrinth of the World and the Paradise of the Heart*. As I perused both books, I soon found the phrase I was looking for: the eyeglasses of general deception, which present all things to your view upside down – and which I, too, had worn until they were removed from my eyes on the snow-covered field, forcing me to see my life for the first time in its true perspective. Surely this is what Mother had meant in remarking that I had a skewed outlook on life. My revulsion and sorrow over how those glasses had distorted my behavior had prompted me to do my utmost not to put them back on, as that well-meaning psychiatrist in New York and my friend Annette had tried to do. I was determined to remain ever alert for the symptoms associated with having my vision dis-torted and returning to my former ways. This didn't mean I cowered with fear whenever I encountered some distinctive woman walking by in the street. Even with Barbara at my side, I was liable to bestow a second glance, perhaps even turn my head, as I would have at virtually any extraordinary sight, whether a noteworthy building, a striking store window display, and for that matter, virtually any dog passing by. Had I become indifferent to the various enticements of this world, no matter in what form, Barbara would have been concerned, not unlike my mother had been, that I might be ill in some peculiar way.

In continuing to peruse Comenius's books, I savored the pervasive common sense reflected in his words: "Let your religion consist in serving me quietly, and in freedom from ceremonies, for I do not require them of you," Comenius cited the enlightener of his soul as advising him. "When you serve me as I teach you, in spirit and in truth, do not quarrel about your religion with anyone, even if they should call you a hypocrite, a heretic or what not."

Another of Comenius's precepts sounded especially familiar. "If someone has a little more purer light and truth, bring it forth, so that from all these pieces of partial truths arises one big, universal TRUTH." My Laguna Beach friend Kenny said it not quite so elegantly but no less forcefully. "When all these people with truth bump into people with truth, then they're all filled with it. And before you know it truth is established on the face of the earth . . . and then we can get on with the new Earth and the New Heaven."

Comenius was putting his thoughts on paper amid great economic chaos and personal tragedy. His *Labyrinth of the World and the Paradise of the Heart* was written shortly after his home in Bohemia had been plundered and burned by Spanish troops, and his wife and two children succumbed in the ensuing pestilence.

No wonder that when Comenius's enlightenment about the true state of human affairs came, his redemptive prescription entailed a complete withdrawal into that paradise of the heart.

This didn't stop Comenius from trying to improve conditions on earth. He dedicated the remaining four decades of his life to reforming education, espousing the radical idea that schools should be made available also to girls – and that learning should be fun. His other focus was trying to find the best way to redirect those human proclivities that led to the sort of wrenching disasters he had experienced. That's what caused him to lament, "If we're destined to wise up eventually, why not wise up now?" Three centuries later, Comenius's precepts for maintaining peace among nations influenced the writing of the charter of the United Nations.

I saw no conflict in Comenius's endeavors to straddle the spiritual and materialistic realms. Despite the grateful optimism with which I approached daily life, his overarching pessimism about our human condition was something I could relate to. How vividly I still recalled my own bleak outlook on the world following that unexpected excoriation from beyond, when my glasses of deception had been summarily removed! Nothing in my life had been more real and influenced me more than that experience on the snow-covered field – except, of course, for the joyous enlightenment that had unexpectedly descended on me in Laguna Beach.

"I have wandered about not knowing where to go," Comenius wrote in the book's concluding paean to his enlightener and redeemer, "but Thou hast overtaken me and hast returned me to myself as well as to Thee."

5/

COUNTRY'S OLDEST ARISTOCRAT DIES AT 98 – that was the headline for the story in the Prague Post, illustrated with a photograph of Father astride one of his machines in his prime as Mr. Exercycle.

I returned to Prague as promptly as I could to help with the funeral arrangements. I was grateful that only two months earlier, I had been able to spend several weeks with Father in connection with the publication of the final part of my trilogy. On my last evening there, when I looked in on him in his bedroom, he asked me to feel his hands and feet and tell him if I didn't think they were unusually cold. Indeed they were, but since I didn't want to say anything that could upset him, I made no comment. "Oh, that's all right, I know I'm coming to the end of the road," Father rejoined in a calm voice. "Yes, the end of a long, long road. But there's no reason to be sad. I'm satisfied I've done all I can."

Now, two black suited attendants wheeled the refrigerated body into the tiny hospital room reeking of formaldehyde, and silently took their leave. Father was lying fully clad on a canvas stretcher on top of what had once been an operating table. It was strange to behold so irrevocably stiff those ever-expressive family features that I had so noticeably shared – the sloping forehead and the prominent nose with a slight cleft at the tip. Nothing could reanimate them now. As I placed my hand on Father's ice-cold forehead, the realization that this also was the end of the long, long road he and I had traveled together gripped me with the anguish of an irreversible loss.

As was the case with Mother's funeral, I accompanied my younger brother to check on the preparations at the family tomb in the village where Father had been born. Tom had inherited

Father's chauffeur, Vladimir, whose lingering fame as the country's top automobile racer a quarter century ago was as much of an advantage when blundering into a speed trap as volunteering that his passenger was Mr. Count. Watching Tom from the back seat chatting with Vladimir, I had to remind myself that my brother was now one of the country's wealthiest residents. No longer the carefree camera-director from Miami Beach, he was a gaunt, graying man with Mother's worried mien, who had aged markedly over the past three years. I had reluctantly come to realize that our lifelong relationship no longer felt the same because of Tom's evident fear that I might grasp the property offer Father was periodically dangling before me.

The final detail to be resolved was the matter of eulogies: whom to select, without slighting anyone, from among the country's cultural leaders, politicians of various stripes, and Father's leading employees vying to eulogize the Count. The fact that the January weather had converted the unheated church into a freezer box, combined with the custom of seemingly endless oratory, could have turned the service into an ordeal. Our solution was that only my brother and I would speak, and very briefly at that. But the evening before the funeral, Tom ate something at the family banquet that didn't agree with him and spent the night throwing up. The following morning, after dozing off on the front seat next to Vladimir, he awoke about twenty kilometers from our destination, turned to me, and said, "You can have my time."

Although we arrived at the village church with a half-hour to spare, we had to wend our way through the crowded aisles to the apse where our family members were gathering. That put us only a few steps from Father's simple wooden coffin, flanked by an honor guard of a half dozen of his foresters dressed in green, and

193

a dozen local firemen in blue, their breath condensing into individual puffs of mist. Behind them at attention were four senior members of a national athletic organization, braving the cold in the tan shorts and short-sleeved shirts Father had financed.

Everyone in the church remained standing. It may have been because they were enthralled by the pervasive sense of history, which seemed to meld them into a single entity; a more practical reason was that if those who had managed to secure a place in the pews sat down, their view would have been obliterated by the standees. As it was, the bishop serving the mass and his four assisting priests had barely enough room in front of the baroque altar to carry out the rites.

Standing slightly apart from everyone else next to Tom at the edge of the elevated part of the apse, I listened sporadically to the bishop's homily exhorting the people who filled the church to pray that God quickly admit Father's departed soul to heaven. I was mentally trying to go over my unwritten text and impress on my memory the Czech words I intended to use. The one phrase I would repeat in English for our relatives and friends who didn't speak Czech was Father's farewell, I'm coming to the end of the road, yes, the end of a long, long road. But there's no reason to be sad. I'm satisfied I've done all I can. And that he had done, including putting his life on the line to do what he felt he absolutely must, and having worked selflessly to insure the future of his children. Perhaps Father had done God's will when it really counted, and whatever transgressions he may have committed or church mandates disregarded amounted to barely visible blemishes on an otherwise sparkling soul. Was that why Father seemed to have been so miraculously at peace? Yes indeed, I kept repeating to myself, there's no reason to be sad.

By the time I positioned myself behind Father's coffin, I felt composed. "Some ninety eight years ago, in this church, just about in the area where I'm standing now," I began, "a small group of people gathered to christen a newborn. The mayor assures me they used the same pewter christening urn a few steps to my left behind some of our guests. The year was eighteen-ninety-seven, the times were more orderly, and one could pretty much predict the course of life for a newborn, especially for a child coming into the privileged circumstances of a Turner-of-the-Wheel."

I paused to scan the surrounding array of faces and register momentary acknowledgment in the eyes of the people I personally knew. They were letting me know that they recognized the incredible turn of fate that had twisted and enriched my father's life from the course it had been meant to take. I raised my arms to encompass everyone in the church and pose a collective query: "Who could then have imagined what journey lay ahead for this newborn before he would return to be here with us today!" With that I placed both hands on Father's casket, as if to enfold his life and the century it had spanned.

After the mass, an elderly village woman approached me in a huff. "What gall, that bishop," she scoffed, "to think that Mr. Count needs our prayers to get to Heaven!"

EPILOGUE
2021

Within two months of Father's passing, Barbara and I were married — and have now been the beneficiaries of stimulating harmony for more than thirty years. Her constant presence in my life provides an indispensable balm while struggling with past regrets and tussling with daily shortcomings.

My younger brother Tom survived my older brother's legal challenge to his inheritance and remained one of the country's wealthiest men for eight years. By the time he died in 2004, Tom had fulfilled Father's wish, having sired two children with a woman close to half his age, who brought him increasing grief. And as had been Tom's intent in leaving no will, his underage progeny under Czech law inherited the entire estate, with their mother appointed as executor. In that capacity, she terminated the Theater's twenty-year gifting lease, despite the ten-year extension my brother had provided on his deathbed in a written note. Having legally adopted our family name, she has used the power of her new wealth to portray Tom's two children as Father's sole descendants representing the family's historic line. Sic transit gloria mundi.

As for my sister Manya, she never gave up her efforts to bring me back into the fold, praying for me and cautiously broaching the subject in our weekly telephone conversations and whenever we would meet during summers on the Cape. Unswerving in her faith, she at times left me wishing I could have her certitude.

In surveying the long arc of what I had experienced, I have been increasingly intrigued by the guiding universal hand that had so miraculously kept my father safe in his perilous drives to Boston, no less miraculously brought Barbara into my life, and countless times ensured I would come out on the right side of potentially life-changing situations. I shudder to think, for instance, how I might have been kicked out of Yale, ended my Naval career in jail, or caused someone's death, including my own, through unwitting heedlessness. Was this the guiding hand of one or more members of the Trinity, each of whom I had experienced in such an individualistic way, or was it what passes for fate, whose workings for better or for worse are as unfathomable as trying to imagine a black hole in the center of our milky way that is more than four million times the mass of the sun in a universe of at least a hundred thousand million other galaxies, some with black holes several thousand million times the mass of our sun.

And how about the coming of the new reality, the new paradigm, the New Heaven and the New Earth – and as prophesied in Revelations, that God would then make his home with mankind?

A universally overlooked detail in the Gospel of St. John may provide a clue. On the eve of his martyrdom, Jesus reportedly promised his distraught disciples that he would send them a Helper Spirit. "The Helper, the Holy Spirit, whom the Father will send in my name," Jesus said, "will teach you everything and make you remember all that I have told you." Though used interchangeably, this Helper Spirit is not exactly the same as the traditional Holy Spirit, whose most notable presence during Jesus's earthly life was in the form of the descending dove at the time of his baptism. The Helper Spirit, however, wouldn't become available until *after* Jesus had completed his mission on earth. "If I do not go," Jesus explained to his small group of simple men unwilling to face the loss of their master, "the Helper will not come to you. But if I do go away, then I will send him [it*] to you."

In our technology-oriented world, the foregoing evokes an image of Jesus ascending to his heavenly base and having to activate in some mysterious way a program tantamount to remote learning. Scheduled to coincide with one of Jerusalem's large feasts, the day of the Pentecost, the inaugural manifestation of the Helper Spirit was a *son et lumière* event, replete with whooshing sounds and flaming lights. Imbued with the Holy [Helper] Spirit, the disciples suddenly found themselves able to converse in the many languages of the foreigners that had come to Jerusalem for this occasion. While some among the milling crowds were amazed and confused by what they had witnessed, others made fun of them, saying they were merely drunk. But as the disciple Peter pointed out, "These people are not drunk, as you suppose; it is only nine o'clock in the morning."

Was it the Helper Spirit in a different guise that had unexpectedly swooped down on me one morning while strolling along the ocean's edge in Laguna Beach? Was it the Helper Spirit, the new form of the Holy Spirit that Jesus could send only after he had gone "away," which left me suffused with an overwhelming gratitude, a blithesome light-headedness, knowing that with Jesus at my side no travail would be too onerous to bear?

No, I wasn't drunk; it was still morning and the coastal fog was only now beginning to lift. Moreover, my experience of having just been "born again" [from above*] was hardly unique and has been shared by countless millions in our neighborhoods and around the globe. Incomparably more consequential to note is that during his earthly life, Jesus had given the Spirit, in whatever form, unequivocal primacy. "And so I tell you, every sin and blasphemy will be forgiven," he is cited in the Gospel of St.

Mathew, "but blasphemy against the Spirit will not be forgiven. Whoever speaks a word against the Son of Man [Jesus] will be forgiven, but whoever speaks against the Holy Spirit will not be forgiven, either in this age or in the one to come."

Why would Jesus assign such a distinction to the Spirit even at his own belittlement? Was it because Jesus would be wholly reliant on this ethereal entity to continue his work after he had gone "away?" Had Jesus in one sense been acting as an advance emissary, laying the groundwork for the Spirit's coming role? Did the Spirit – whether Helper or one of the traditional versions harkening back to the Old Testament – represent a sort of transmission network, beyond detection by our latest means, whereby the powers "above" have been communicating and interacting with us here "below"? Was it within this network that Jesus had secured a new, dedicated line that would enable him to cultivate and spread "to the ends of the earth" what he had sown – and thus bring about a new age?

Has our civilization now reached the stage when that which has heretofore been concealed in mystery is about to be revealed in a way that will make even unbelievers pay heed? As Neil Armstrong, who is said to have had a mystical experience during his lunar mission, cryptically observed with evident emotion in his last public speech at the White House, "There are great ideas undiscovered, breakthroughs available to those who can remove one of truth's protective layers."

With our civilization teetering on the edge, will this protective layer be removed before it is too late?

*Based on Google-enabled comparisons with original Greek text.
Citations from Good News Bible published by American Bible Society.

AUTHOR'S NOTE

In this autobiographical work, some names and details have been changed for reasons of privacy; other details have been modified to present events and dialogue within a novelistic mold, without compromising the essence of what took place. This is not to say that a harsher as well as a kinder version couldn't be compiled.

An earlier version of this work was published in the Czech Republic as the third volume of a best-selling trilogy. A unified version of that trilogy has been published in the United States as *Confessions of a Hapless Hedonist*.

My thanks to Natalie Chapman for introducing me to the finer elements of style, and to John Hersey for continuing that task in the final years of his life.

.